T5-CAE-467

VGM Opportunities Series

OPPORTUNITIES IN
FITNESS CAREERS

Mary Miller, R.N.P.

Revised by
Lewis R. Baratz, Ph.D.

Foreword by
Kathie Davis
Executive Director
IDEA

**VGM Career Horizons**
a division of *NTC Publishing Group*
Lincolnwood, Illinois USA

Cover Photo Credits

Upper left courtesy of Cybex International, Inc.; upper right courtesy of Elmhurst College, Elmhurst, Illinois; lower left and lower right courtesy of The Cooper Aerobics Center, Dallas, Texas.

331.76090
M64

Library of Congress Cataloging-in-Publication Data

Miller, Mary
    Opportunities in fitness careers / Mary Miller, Lewis R. Baratz.—
—[2nd, rev. ed.]
      p. cm.
    Previously published: Opportunities in fitness careers / Jean
Rosenbaum, Mary Miller. 1967.
    Includes index.
    ISBN 0-8442-4686-7 (hc : alk. paper). — ISBN
0-8442-4687-5 (pbk. : alk. paper).
    1. Physical education and training—Vocational guidance—United
States. 2. Physical therapy—Vocational guidance—United States.
3. Physical fitness—United States. 4. Exercise—United States.
I. Baratz, Lewis. II. Rosenbaum, Jean. Opportunities in fitness
careers. III. Title.
GV481.4.M55   1997   96-48293
                                               CIP

Published by VGM Career Horizons, a division of NTC Publishing Group
4255 West Touhy Avenue
Lincolnwood (Chicago), Illinois 60646-1975, U.S.A.
© 1997 by NTC Publishing Group. All rights reserved.
No part of this book may be reproduced, stored in a retrieval
system, or transmitted in any form or by any means,
electronic, mechanical, photocopying, recording or otherwise,
without the prior permission of NTC Publishing Group.
Manufactured in the United States of America.

7 8 9 0 VP 9 8 7 6 5 4 3 2 1

CONTENTS

The fitness instructor. Teaching guidelines for the
multilevel class. Exercise do's and don't's. Monitoring
the heart rate. Medical and rehabilitative options.

Group-exercise or aerobics instructor. Corporate fitness
instructor. Group and personal trainers. Nautilus instructor.
Exercise physiologist. Yoga instructor.

Osteopathic Physician (D.O.). Physician (M.D.). Doctor
of Chiropractic (D.C).

ABOUT THE AUTHORS

Mary Miller, R.N.P., a registered nurse practitioner, is the Associate Director of the American Aerobics Association (AAA). She has been an involved fitness advocate for more than fifteen years. Mary has taught yoga to all ages, and designed and conducted a special yoga program for psychiatric patients. Mary has established and taught prenatal exercise programs for health clubs and co-organized and taught AAA aerobic programs for healthy and medically impaired individuals. She has written articles on aerobics and women's health care, and has been a consultant and host for many medical and educational films for nurses, mothers, and exercisers, including *Aerobics on the Easy Side, A New Mother's Feelings,* and *Sports Medicine.*

Lewis R. Baratz, Ph.D., writer, cultural historian, applications developer, and management consultant, is the author of VGM's *Guide to Temporary Employment* and is the "Healthtips from Yesteryear" columnist for *Exercise for Men Only.* Lewis has prepared this second revised edition of *Opportunities in Fitness Careers.*

ACKNOWLEDGMENTS

The authors wish to extend a very special thanks to the following organizations for providing some of the information for this book. They are: The Aerobics Center; IDEA, The International Association of Fitness Professionals; Jazzercise; and Rockwell International.

We would also like to thank the American College of Sports Medicine, the American Heart Association, the National Therapeutic Recreation Society, and all the other organizations that generously shared statistical and other data.

FOREWORD

The revolution is calling you.

Few factors are as effective at building a healthy world as is regular physical activity. And that means that few other careers can offer you a greater opportunity to make a difference in people's lives as can one in fitness.

It's a high calling; fitness professionals are no longer about leg warmers, hip-hop music, and high-impact aerobics. What we have experienced in the fitness industry since it's beginnings in the late 1960s accounts for nothing short of a fantastic revolution in growth, professionalism, and respect.

More people than ever before have turned to personal fitness trainers and group exercise instructors for guidance and support as they strive for new ways to live, feel, and look better.

And the more society learns about the preventive benefits of health and fitness, the more government and the medical community recognize the incredible value of physical activity, the louder the revolution calls you to take your place.

Whether you come as a group exercise instructor, a personal fitness trainer, a health club manager, a physical education instructor, an athletic trainer, an athletic coach, or any of the countless other specialties in fitness you'll read about in this book, there is room for you—if you want to make a difference.

This book will illuminate countless doorways—all of them leading to a bright future, all of them vital as you prepare to do your part to keep the revolution alive.

We greet you with open arms. Welcome to the revolution.

Kathie Davis
Executive Director and Co-Founder
IDEA, The International Association
of Fitness Professionals

INTRODUCTION

A career in health and fitness offers immense personal accomplishment. There's enormous interaction with other people, whether it be in a clinical, outdoor, group, or one-on-one setting. Most professionals working in the health and fitness fields are themselves health-conscious and take every opportunity to keep in shape and shun the poisons that today's diet and lifestyle have to offer. With so many opportunities to choose from, the aspiring health and fitness professional may feel overwhelmed. The goal of this book is to help the novice health and fitness career shopper gain some insight and structure in her or his quest for the ideal opportunity in health and fitness.

What immediately comes to mind is just what is meant by "health and fitness"? By defining the term, the scope of this book becomes clear. To consider health and fitness as two distinct entities would necessitate a significantly more voluminous work that explores opportunities in all aspects of the health-care industry, including research, delivery, and business aspects, each of which is a book in itself. The fitness portion would include the hands-on, the reparative or therapeutic aspects, and the business end as well. This book considers health and fitness as the singular term "health fitness" and covers the three essential components that lay within this more focused parameter.

We therefore will examine opportunities positioned more on the "health" side (e.g., osteopathic and chiropractic medicine), those on the "fitness" side (e.g., aerobics instructor, personal trainer), and those that bridge the two in their reparative nature (e.g., physical and occupational therapy). The need for qualified, well-trained personnel in all branches of the health fitness industry continues to grow beyond expectations. Health fitness is one of the fastest growing industries in the United States, and the job market it has created is one of the most varied and exciting.

New jobs are being created by the thousands. New books, journals, magazines, and videos come out every month. The health fitness boom has caught the imagination of the American public, with Canada and much of Western Europe and Australia closely following. With such an explosion in interest, the nature of the industry has already changed since this book was first published. The numbers of qualified professionals continue to increase, and salaries are up. As the population ages, the need for specialists in both cardiovascular maintenance and gerontology grows, while a weight-conscious society demands more teachers and trainers. Professional organizations, certification associations, and state licensing boards continue to increase in order to protect the public from charlatans, reward those who excel in their chosen fields, and give an edge in the job search to deserving candidates.

Finally, the advent of the Internet, and especially the Home Page, has impacted the entire industry. Research, affiliation, certification, and training are now merely a few clicks of the mouse away. This revised edition of *Opportunities in Fitness Careers* explores the on-line venue to help you get the tools you need to get going. As you read the career descriptions, focus on the big picture. Ask yourself: Is this career logistically and economically feasible for me? Do I have the right personality and the physical requirements for it? Will it be rewarding to me? Systematically research those careers that excite you, especially those that make you think, "Wow! I could do this all day, every day. And just think, I'll even get paid for it!" Once you obtain the materials you need from colleges, universities, organizations, your local library, or other sources, contact people already working in that field. Ask if you can observe them at work. Find out about the ups, the downs, the perks, and the concerns of their jobs.

I hope we've provided a great access point for you as you explore all the opportunities in fitness careers!

Lewis R. Baratz, Ph.D.

CHAPTER 1

THE PHYSICAL FITNESS BOOM

> The health of the people is really the foundation upon which all their happiness and all their powers as a state depend.

> Benjamin Disraeli

For many thousands of years, people kept physically fit and strong through the exertion involved in finding enough to eat. People's physical nature was served by a life of climbing, leaping, and running in search of food. Men also guarded their precious turf and obtained, kept, and protected their mates through physical means. The women kept fit by working nonstop just to survive.

As society gave way to agriculture, people spent their days planting, tilling, and harvesting crops. At the time of the Industrial Revolution (the early-to-mid 1800s), most manufacturing depended on constant physical effort. Human muscle provided at least one-third of the energy that drove the world's workshops, factories, and farms. Today, muscle power accounts for less than half of that energy expenditure. Though society has changed, altering the workplace, the human body remains the same. People still need regular, vigorous exercise to keep their bodies fit. Unfortunately, today's workplace does not provide the activity to meet our physiological needs. The result has been an increase in the incidence of a number of physical and stress-related ailments associated with a lack of proper activity.

Fortunately, people are becoming increasingly involved with improving their bodies. Health advocates are beginning to recognize that structured exercise and wellness programs are one of the best forms of preventive medicine, something our Canadian neighbors have known for years. Peer pressure to stay fit and trim is everywhere. Some insurance companies are even offering rate reductions to people who participate in health fitness programs.

A major reason for the continued growth of the fitness industry is that more and more people believe that their regular workout helps prevent disease and increases longevity. Also, many exercisers attest that keeping in shape helps them look and feel better. Other factors include the belief that today's adult population has more leisure time than ever before. Additionally, exercise is now an accepted part of rehabilitation programs for heart attack victims and other patients.

The July 1996 *Physical Activity and Health: A Report of the Surgeon General,* released by the Centers for Disease Control (CDC) in collaboration with the President's Council on Physical Fitness and Sports (PCPFS), painted a somewhat grim picture of the nation's health. Only 22 percent of U.S. adults engage in regular, vigorous physical activity, but the news is better for young people. One-half of U.S. young people (ages 12 to 21 years) regularly participate in some form of exercise. Enrollment in physical education classes, however, has declined from approximately 81 percent to 70 percent during the first half of the decade. On the positive side, the immediate need for addressing the situation is clear. Millions of Americans swim, cycle, play basketball or volleyball, or engage in some other sports. Health club memberships continue to increase, with men and women and boys and girls of all ethnic, educational, and socioeconomic backgrounds lifting weights, running, swimming, and participating in aerobics classes. The report made one thing clear: massive health fitness intervention is needed in the schools, the communities, and the workplace.

On the prevention and survival side, there's some good news. Public awareness and intervention have brought mortality from coronary heart disease down more than one-half from just thirty years ago. Technology, of course, is also a major player in this. Stroke-related deaths have declined from 100 victims per 100,000 in 1940 to about 25 per 100,000 today. We're winning the war against hypertension, and rheumatic fever deaths are almost nonexistent in the United States. Cholesterol levels, however, are high in an estimated 52 percent of the adult population, and cardiovascular disease remains the number one killer in the United States for every year but one (1918, the year of the influenza pandemic). More sophisticated technology, including heart transplants, is not the ideal way to go, so health fitness professionals certainly have their work cut out. There is hope, however, as Americans continue to reduce red meat consumption, practice moderation in alcohol intake, toss the cigarettes in the trash, and burn off the extra fat and cholesterol. Fish and meatless dishes are found on virtually every restaurant menu in the country, and bars in all fifty states recognize that a significant percentage of their clientele will order only nonalcoholic drinks. Responsible drinking has become the norm owing both to health consciousness and legal and financial liability.

The benefits of exercise are being recognized by private industry, which loses millions of dollars each year in productivity and real assets to ailments such as the common backache. Several hundred companies now have active exercise programs that are boosting their employees' health as well as their productivity. Work is where most people spend a third of their weekday lives, and it is also the place where most workers *sit* to do their jobs. If employees benefit from a lower risk of heat attack or disability through exercise programs, the employer also gains. The firm that encourages its associates to stay fit, alert, and healthy will not only save money but can position itself more favorably in our highly competitive world.

Individual programs at companies have made the following reports:

- Ontario, Canada Health Insurance Plan—"High levels of physical fitness lead to lower medical claims, reduced coronary heart disease."
- Goodyear, Sweden—"Fitness program led to 50 percent reduction in absenteeism."
- NASA—"Fitness program participants had more positive work attitudes, less strain and tension, improved work performance."
- New York State Education Department—"Employee physical fitness program led to reduction of absenteeism and reduction of four risk factors for heart disease."

Some questions about cost-effectiveness have been answered in a study carried out by Dr. Roy Shepard and his associates at the University of Toronto. They reported on the effects of a program in which they studied 1,125 people, more than half the staff of the home offices of two large insurance companies. One company carpeted and painted a 2,700-square-foot space where thirty-minute exercise classes were given two or three times a week. Vigorous recruiting brought more than half the eligible employees to the sessions. At the other company, a matched group of employees were evaluated, but no fitness sessions or facilities were provided. The evaluation measured aerobic power (maximal oxygen intake), flexibility, and body fat content. Employees in the fitness program improved significantly, but not dramatically, on all these scores. Given the brief period of time devoted to aerobic exercise, only modest changes could have been expected. Certain other benefits to employer and employee were striking. In particular, absentee rates went down in the company with the program. Monday and Friday absences alone went down 22 percent. For a company of 1,400 employees, comparable in size to the ones studied, Shepard calculated there would be 3,500 fewer lost days, which is equivalent to more than $175,000 in salary costs saved.

There were indications of other, larger savings as well. Shepard's study found that employees participating in the fitness program tended to stay with the company. Their turnover rate was only 1.5 percent compared with 15 percent among nonparticipants at the same company and all employees at the other. Because the cost of hiring and training a new employee is high, about $6,300, this finding suggested an annual savings of more than $500,000 for the company with the fitness program. Participants felt more alert, enjoyed work more, and reported better relationships with fellow workers. A full two-thirds felt more relaxed, more patient, and less fatigued during the workday.

Xerox, IBM, the federal government, and thousands of other companies and institutions have maintained employee fitness centers. The result across the board has been greater employee moral; fewer days off for backaches, colds, and minor ailments; and greater employee productivity and retention. Many companies have also benefited from lower insurance premiums associated with a greater degree of "wellness" among their employees.

Hundreds of companies specializing in fitness products have suddenly appeared. Profit margins at the retail level in the various segments of the fitness industry can be as high as 45 percent. The fitness industry is utilizing the television media with advertising. For instance, Soloflex spent $1 million to advertise on network television. Nautilus paid $500,000 a week for TV advertising with commercials for home machines featuring Terri Jones, wife of Nautilus founder Arthur Jones. Other companies selectively target audiences by advertising on certain TV stations and at particular times of the day. The fitness lifestyle emphasizes trendy new equipment and designer clothes, and there's little sign that the market has peaked. The industry continues to come up with new products that keep people interested, and more people continue to join the movement.

Health fitness is exploding as a global industry, and this fast growth rate is creating many opportunities for you. The statements in the following paragraphs were made by knowledgeable people and organizations about improving health.

> American Health Foundation, New York—"A growing consensus among health experts sees ours as a legacy of a medical system which provides too much care, too late . . . a system which is failing because it meets the patient when he is already diseased."

> U.S. Public Health Service—"Habitual inactivity is thought to contribute to hypertension, chronic fatigue . . . premature aging, the poor musculature . . . which are the

major causes of lower back pain and injury, mental tension, coronary heart disease, and obesity."

Daniel Kosich, Ph.D., senior director for professional development at IDEA, The International Association of Fitness Professionals, and author of *Get Real: A Personal Guide to Real-Life Weight Management*—"Americans spend over $33 billion *every year* on weight loss pills, potions, and powders, yet every year more and more of us are obese. For reasons ranging from our need to cut the national deficit and control health care costs to our desire to live healthier, happier, longer lives, we simply must get fitter as a nation."

Kenneth H. Cooper, M.D., M.P.H., Founder and Director of the Cooper Clinic, Dallas, Texas—"Heart disease is the most common cause of death in men 35–54 years of age. But with proper weight, proper diet, and proper exercise, deaths from heart disease can be lowered. The highest price paid for poor health is in the suffering and just plain lack of joy that illness and accidents impose on victims and members of their families...."

Richard E. Palmer, M.D., former president, American Medical Association—"The medical system affects about 10 percent of the usual factors that determine a patient's state of health...the remaining 90 percent are determined by factors over which doctors have little or no control. Physicians maintain that more sensible personal health decisions on smoking, drinking, exercise, proper diet, and such, offer a better hope for a healthier American than...the medical system."

The Wall Street Journal—"The next major advance in the health of the American people will result only from what the individual is willing to do for himself."

CDC's National Physical Activity Initiative—"Regular physical activity offers substantial improvements in health and well-being for the majority of Americans, who are not receiving enough physical activity. Moderate physical activity performed on most days of the week can substantially reduce the risk of dying from heart disease, the leading cause of death in the United States, and can reduce the risk of developing colon cancer, diabetes, and high blood pressure. Currently, more than 60 percent of American adults are not regularly active, and 25 percent of the adult population is not active at all."

It's mostly about lifestyle. Of course, environmental and genetic factors cannot be overlooked, but taking control can reduce or in some instances nullify any inherited negative traits. There's still much that can be done to lower risk for heart attack, strokes, and hypertension. Obesity, while recognized by the Equal Employment Commission as constituting an impairment as defined by the Americans with Disabilities Act (ADA) of 1992 and put into effect in 1994, can often be controlled through a strict medical program developed by specialists including physicians, nutritionists, and also mental-health providers, if habit and low-esteem are significant contributing factors. Were it not for our fast-paced, pass-the-buck habits, the incidence of auto injuries and fatalities would decline. Back problems, too, one of the leading causes of "sick days" from work, would be less of a problem and the same would hold true for eye strain, osteoporosis, and the like.

Companies are more than willing—in fact, under ADA they're obliged—to provide ergonomic workstations to anyone who asks, in order to prevent serious back problems and the plague of the nineties, repetitive stress injury, especially the dreaded Carpal Tunnel Syndrome.

With the real and critical need for intervention, the earnest desire of many millions of people for guidance, and the projected openings for rehabilitative health professionals that an aging population and technology-oriented society demands, the opportunities and the choices in health fitness are many.

CHAPTER 2

AN EXPLODING, NEW, INDEPENDENT PROFESSION

Happiness lies, first of all, in health.

G. W. Curtis

In February 1961, the Department of Health, Education, and Welfare held an unprecedented Conference on Youth Fitness. Today, thirty-five years later, there has been a great awakening to the fitness movement. Nearly all fifty states have their own state physical fitness organizations with the state head of physical fitness serving as a governor's appointee. As a result of the movement begun at the 1961 conference, physical fitness activities are now available to all students, including the physically, mentally, and emotionally challenged. Many organizations are also pushing for physical fitness of adults, encouraging all of us to become more physically active.

The physical fitness movement has motivated many organizations to open exercise rooms or gyms. Clients are flocking to these facilities, often without the experience or knowledge to help them choose wisely and take advantage of what the facility may have to offer. Some of the "trainers" and "instructors" are adequately prepared, but others, unfortunately, are opportunists lacking in the background necessary to teach a safe fitness program.

The great popularity of the health fitness movement has made physical education appealing to primary schoolchildren and college students. Now, instead of taking "boring gym classes," they can enroll in dance, swimming, gymnastics, aerobics, aquatics, "Jazzercise," weight training, running, and various sports. The Rehabilitation Act of 1973 called for every disadvantaged child to be granted a public school education equal to all students, specifically referring to physical education and sports. The more recent Americans with Disability Act and subsequent and pending legislation extend that guarantee to all persons. Special courses for teaching these individuals are increasing markedly in physical education professional training departments as the demands for such special teachers increase.

Many health fitness advocates have made the public more health conscious by promoting and participating in fitness programs themselves. Dr. Kenneth Cooper, physician, public health advocate, teacher, writer, and director of the Cooper Clinic in Dallas, Texas, developed the concept of determining a person's current fitness status and from that tailoring a training regimen to improve overall physical condition and cardiac efficiency. Jacki Sorensen, known as the "Grandmother of Aerobics," used the knowledge she gained from Dr. Cooper's book, *The Aerobics Program for Total Well-Being* (1982) to develop her dance exercise course, which had its beginning on a televised fitness program at the United States Air Force base in Puerto Rico. Lenore R. Zohman, M.D., one of the most famous exercise cardiologists in the world, has successfully used aerobic dance in cardiac rehabilitation. Exercise pioneer Jack LaLanne brought health and fitness right into the living room of Cold War–era America.

Many celebrities have become models of fitness, exuding their enthusiasm for exercise via the media. Richard Simmons, Jane Fonda, Cher, Christie Brinkley, Tony Cacciotti, Linda Evans, Racquel Welch, and Victoria Principal, to name just a few, have approached the public with books and videotapes on their techniques toward a "healthier you." The list seems to be growing overnight, and local video rental establishments stock exercise videos that target every body part, literally from top to bottom.

The fitness industry in America includes a multitude of new equipment, high technology, books, magazines, television, and videocassettes. A trainer today must be equipped not only with the basic knowledge of anatomy and physiology, but also with sophisticated knowledge of the industry and the ability to communicate as well. The training and education necessary to this expanding field is discussed in Chapter 6.

CHAPTER 3

TRENDS AFFECTING
HEALTH FITNESS CAREERS

The first wealth is health.

Ralph Waldo Emerson

In the last thirty years, health clubs and suppliers of specialized health and fitness equipment have matured. Clubs that once offered only golf have added swimming, tennis, saunas, exercise rooms, and aerobics machines. There is a marked shift toward social sports in exercise facilities. Changes are occurring in special services. For example, boxing programs have virtually been replaced by Nautilus machines and fitness conditioning centers. Free weights, flat and inclined benches, and aerobics equipment such as jogging machines and stairclimbers, are now a staple in even the most modest of clubs. Swimming provides the opportunity to enjoy an exercise program that gives the same muscle toning and cardiovascular benefit derived from other forms of exercise.

The fitness industry has flourished without the constraint of federal guidelines or regulation, for better or worse. With the notable exception of the medical and rehabilitative sides of the industry, much is self-regulated. As such, the industry has endeavored to develop and improve its standards. However, a large number of facilities still engage in unsafe practices. Therefore, you should examine the facility closely before accepting a job.

Only a few years ago, athletes without any real specialization were hired for positions in health clubs. Now many health fitness employees have specialized training in health and physical education, sports administration, and exercise physiology. Many have bachelor's and master's degrees. The industry needs people with backgrounds in early childhood education, aquatics, physiology, and kinesiology (the study of the principles of body mechanics and anatomy of human movement). A bachelor's degree may be more a stepping-stone in the professional careers of those in the public sector than for those in the private sector. In some areas of the public sector, a master's degree is mandatory for upper-level positions. Continuing education, either in an academic setting or through seminars and courses offered by professional associations, has become an important aspect of career advancement for many in managed health fitness.

One important side effect of industry growth is the increased employment opportunity. Thousands of new jobs have opened up. Some of these are full-time positions, while others may provide work only a few nights a week. Both full-time and part-time career opportunities are expected to increase during the next decade. The explosion in technology also demands new and more sophisticated professionals. From weight trainers to aerobics instructors to recreation leaders to repetitive-stress-injury therapists, the health fitness industry is among the fastest-growing employment sector today. So, let's jump on the health fitness bandwagon and explore the opportunities available.

CHAPTER 4

EXPLORING THE OPTIONS

There is a wide range of career opportunities available to those interested in the fitness field. Many professionals, such as *physicians, therapists,* and *fitness counselors,* work with people to develop exercise and nutrition programs. Professionals may specialize, as in the case of those who work exclusively with young children or the elderly. Others may work with all types of people.

Before you embark on a career in health fitness, you should first closely examine your motivation for going into the field. Many people choose an occupation in this field because they are committed to fitness. They enjoy being physically fit and want to share this experience. Others opt for the "health" side, i.e., the medical aspect of the industry, and go on to become osteopathic or chiropractic providers. A significant number of people choose the rehabilitative or therapeutic side and work as occupational, physical, and recreational therapists.

THE FITNESS INSTRUCTOR

Today's fitness instructor is a disciplined athlete who can set an excellent example for clients. Being an instructor involves more than just an interest in people and health. Health fitness specialists need training in physical education and exercise physiology. Good health and stamina, a pleasant personality, and the desire to help others are also necessary qualities for a health fitness career. Aspirants should have an interest in working with people of all ages, backgrounds, and abilities. They should possess the gift of inspiring confidence in others. Additional qualifications include emotional stability and maturity, a keen sense of humor, patience, ingenuity, and the ability to express oneself clearly both orally and in writing.

To use the industry vernacular, an *instructor* is one who works usually with a group in a more-or-less structured environment. Someone who teaches an aerobics class is thus an aerobics instructor. A *trainer* tends to work on a one-on-one basis with clients, often on a freelance basis, and is generally associated with weight lifting or gymnastics, where a clear-cut goal is sought. A *coach* is someone who prepares a team or a professional athlete to meet a specific objective, such as placing in the Olympics.

The fitness instructor's place of employment is varied. You might work in a large or small corporate or industrial firm's fitness center, a nursing home, preschool, hospital, dance studio, private club, community fitness center, or even on a cruise ship. There are a few areas in the industry in which you do not have to be a participant or maintain contact activity with clients. For example, you can be a wellness promoter by designing and/or managing programs, utilizing skills attained in business administration classes.

You should ask yourself several questions before embarking upon a career in health fitness. The aspiring trainer and instructor should consider the following:

1. Do I have the self-confidence and leadership skills to motivate others?
2. Am I comfortable working with a variety of client types and ages?
3. Do I assume responsibility for professional self-evaluation?
4. Do I understand how to create a safe class?
5. Do I have an understanding of anatomy and physiology?
6. Am I certified in CPR (cardiopulmonary resuscitation)?
7. Do I have an adequate educational background to screen clients for health problems?
8. Am I adequately trained in my area?
9. Am I a physically fit role model for students?

TEACHING GUIDELINES
FOR THE MULTILEVEL CLASS

You may at some time find yourself in a teaching position in which there are students of various levels of fitness. This is especially true in businesses that have one program for all their employees. Below are helpful guidelines to help you avoid the common pitfalls of a multilevel class.

1. Obtain written permission from any student that has a medical problem before allowing her or him to participate in your class.
2. Always give a review of the class format, stressing a non-competitive atmosphere.
3. Remind participants during sessions to "listen to their bodies."

4. Give students specific instructions on how to pace themselves and breathe and move properly.

5. Easily fatigued beginning exercise students need constant encouragement, especially so they do not feel they cannot keep up with others.

6. A person who is overweight or has low self-esteem should be treated sensitively and given lots of motivation, support, and reassurance.

7. Some intermediate students go overboard and others barely push themselves. Your responsibility is to assist each one to reach her or his highest training level without injury. Offer them hand or leg weights, if appropriate, to enhance cardiovascular output.

8. The advanced students, who are often bored in an intermediate class, can be further stimulated by periodically offering them advice and means toward improving body alignment and control with each movement.

9. Advanced students should be instructed to rest a day between strenuous workouts. This group tends toward a high level of injuries due to overuse of the body.

10. Exercise in front of your students until many are familiar with the routines. Eliminate boredom by having an intermediate or advanced student lead a routine. This will permit you the time to circulate through your class, motivating, adjusting, and encouraging your participants.

11. If you are unable to leave the front of the room, make eye-to-eye contact with students who need your attention to encourage or pace them.

Before embarking on a career as a health fitness instructor, try attending various types of classes at different clubs and organizations. There are so many to choose from today. You will find many of these clubs and organizations listed in the *Yellow Pages* under "physical fitness programs." There are also many other health fitness related opportunities listed in other VGM Career Horizons Series books, such as *Opportunities in Nutrition Careers, Opportunities in Sports and Athletics, Opportunities in Sports Medicine,* and *Opportunities in Recreation and Leisure Careers.*

EXERCISE DO'S AND DON'T'S

What danger can occur from improper exercise technique? Plenty. The main danger is injury to the lower back and knees. Incorrect or quick, uncontrolled movement can compress the back and strain the knees. Exercise benefits can be sabotaged when specific muscle groups are not worked at all effectively. Many people in your class are so busy trying to keep up, that they forget to breathe or to check their body for proper alignment. Fitness instructors *must* teach proper body positions during exercise.

The following steps should help you guide your students toward executing proper technique during exercise.

1. Make sure initial posture position is correct before beginning to move.
2. The body must stay balanced throughout the movement and should continue to be aligned, especially at the knees and pelvis. The knees *always* bend over the toes, and there should be no hyperextension of the back.
3. Relax all body parts not specifically involved in the exercise. This reduces muscular tension and conserves energy.

4. Don't jump side-to-side on one foot. This may cause torn ligaments or fractures.

5. Don't jump so high that both feet are more than six inches off the ground at the same time. The shock of landing increases the risk of injury.

6. Remember to breathe! During stretching, breathe in and out, rhythmically. For example, when stretching up, breathe in. When bending over, breathe out.

7. Stretching should follow a period of walking around a little to get the body warmed up. Warm muscles stretch 30 percent more than cold muscles. A cold muscle, due to its limited performance abilities, can easily be damaged.

8. During stretching, never bounce or make jerky movements. Stretching should always be slow and easy.

9. Avoid too many continuous movements of any body part, as this burns off all the glycogen (carbohydrates) and causes the accumulation of lactic acid (waste product), which leads to an anaerobic state (lack of oxygen).

10. During the five to ten minutes of peak exercise, participants' heart rates should reach 80 percent of their age-specific maximums (see next section).

11. Never do aerobics in bare feet.

Make sure your program is progressive. It should be one that challenges participants of every skill level without demanding too much of beginners. Instructors should encourage students to build up to the full routine gradually. Flexibility, endurance, strength, and muscle tone will come, but they take time. When students feel they've reached their limits, instructors should not pressure them to do more.

MONITORING THE HEART RATE

A good method for gauging cardiovascular fitness is heart rate monitoring. This reliable measure should be incorporated into all exercise sessions. Heart rates should be taken before, during, and after exercise sessions. This will ensure the minimal effort necessary for benefit but avoid overly strenuous levels of exercise. Note that the very first monitoring should be done by your client's physician before he or she starts to train with you. It's not just seemingly healthy people over the age of thirty-five who should be certified fit for exercise, but everyone. In fact, in August 1996 the American Heart Association, for the first time, set national recommendations for screening high school and college athletes for heart ailments, particularly hypertrophic cardiomyopathy, an enlargement of the heart muscle that has led to the sudden death of seemingly healthy young people. As a trainer, it is important for you to inform your clients about the need for a physical examination before they start to work with you.

Heart rate monitoring before, during, and after the exercise session is a very simple task. You can use the trusted, old-fashioned method. Lightly apply your index and middle fingers to the radial artery (on the thumb side of the wrist), the temporal artery (in front of and slightly above the ear), the carotid artery (on the neck approximately halfway between the sternal notch and the ear lobe), or the left chest just beneath the breast. It is important to touch the carotid artery only on one side at a time! The number of pulsations or heartbeats is counted over a given time period, usually fifteen seconds. The result is then multiplied by the number required to give beats per minute. For instance, if a student counts to twenty in fifteen seconds, the pulse rate would be eighty.

Another method is the electronic sensor. Electronic sensors are devices students can purchase for use on their own. Prices vary from $40 to $400 for the more sophisticated models. A strap is affixed around the chest and the heart rate is transmitted to a device about the size of a beeper, which gives the result. The more sophisticated devices are cordless and also double as pedometers and stopwatches. They can be used during the workout to signal irregularities or over-rapid heart rates.

Because resting and target heart rates are both important indicators of fitness, instructors should lead a heart rate count before the session (resting heart rate), after the aerobic session (target heart rate), and after the cool down period (recovery heart rate). Remember to tell your students when they take the target heart rate pulse never to stop moving. The heart rate needs to be gradually increased, then gradually decreased. Heart rate monitoring can enable the student to adjust the intensity of exercise to achieve optimal conditioning. If the rate falls consistently below the target rate, intensity can be increased, such as by adding hand weights. Naturally, if the target rate is exceeded, the intensity should be decreased. Heart rate monitoring can help avoid overexertion, decrease injuries, and help participants appreciate the physical demands of different exercise activities. Heart rates will usually rise quickly in an unusually warm, humid environment. As an instructor, you should modify sessions as required to keep heart rates within the target zone.

MEDICAL AND REHABILITATIVE OPTIONS

A career as a health care provider requires commitment, plain and simple. There are financial concerns, such as paying for professional education, and also time and logistical matters to consider. Becoming an osteopathic physician, for example, requires a four-year degree, four years of medical school, and one to three years of residency before becoming eligible to sit for a licensure exam. Medical students put in eighteen-hour days studying and making rounds, and the strain can be enormous. Chiropractic training is less rigorous and can be completed in six years. People considering these fields also need certain personal tools. They need maturity and dedication. They also need to achieve a substantial background in physiology, biochemistry, and biomechanics, as well as experience in working with people who may be physically restricted in varying degrees.

Rehabilitative therapists also need training in the sciences, particularly anatomy and biomechanics. For them, however, interpersonal skills are even more essential, because they work intimately with patients and clients. Besides physical, occupational, and recreational therapists, there are assistant- and aide-level positions. These opportunities also require a deep commitment and additional training as the level of sophistication increases. The rewards, however, are great because rehabilitative therapists often see the results of their work and take great pride and pleasure in helping people.

CHAPTER 5

HEALTH FITNESS ON-LINE

So far we've touched on three career tracks in health fitness. The job descriptions and references furnished in this book should give you the start you need to make the career decision that's best for you. If you're savvy, you will write away to various professional societies and organizations for additional information. You should also invest some time exploring the health fitness materials on the Internet to better help you decide on a career path.

If you have a computer at home or have access to a computer, you can reach the Internet through a variety of Internet access carriers such as America Online, CompuServ, or Prodigy. "Surfin' the Net" will give you an excellent idea of the scope and magnitude of the health fitness world. You can use search engines such as *AltaVista, Lycos, Magellan,* and *Yahoo* to find related topics by using the keywords *health, fitness, sports, athletics, wellness, cardiovascular,* and so on. You'll find everything from organization home pages to academic programs to ads for exercise equipment to job postings. To make things easier, this chapter provides some selected websites for you to visit from many thousands in order to learn more about health fitness opportunities.

1. The American Heart Association (AHA)

   http://www.amhrt.org/

   You can obtain important data from the AHA concerning mortality and morbidity, risk factors, and the benefits of a healthy lifestyle. Follow their links to their other sites such as

   http://www.amhrt.org/resources.html

   to view some of their excellent publication sites.

   Likewise, the Surgeon General's Report on the state of physical fitness can be read at:

   http://www.cdc.gov/nccdphp/sgr/sgr.htm

2. The National Association for Human Development (NAHD) The National Association for Human Development provides an interesting Internet site. Data on human potential can be found at:

   http://www.social.com/health/nhic/data/hr0100/ hr0169.html

   The NAHD site provides links to numerous other organizations of interest. Try entering

   http://www.social.com/health/nhic/data

   and have a good look around.

3. Sport Information Research Centre (SIRC) If you are interested in learning about health fitness organizations, conferences, and research opportunities around the globe, aim your computer at Canada. SIRC maintains an

excellent and friendly site. You can visit their home page at:

http://www.sirc.ca/

Make sure you check out their journal listings at

http://www.sirc.ca/usmed.html and
http://www.sirc.ca/infocen.html

4. The Center for Exercise Research at the Department of Kinesiology, Kansas State University, provides a forum for students and professionals to communicate and collaborate on common interests. Interested persons can explore its site at:

http://www-personal.ksu.edu/~kines/CER.html

You should also visit the site at the University of Waterloo for information on this diverse field and its delivery in Canada at:

http://healthy.uwaterloo.ca/kin.html

The University of Waterloo also has an innovative program in ergonomics, which is the science of designing household and workplace items—from chairs and tables to beds and pillows to steering wheels to computer mouses—in such a way as to avoid back, neck, shoulder, leg, or other repetitive strain injury. Their site is:

http://www.ahs.uwaterloo.ca/kin/ergon.html

5. The National Center for Health Fitness (NCHF)
The National Center for Health Fitness provides a significant number of educational programs, health promotion

programs, research and program evaluation, and other services. Members are also privy to an extensive battery of job postings in health fitness. Their home page is:

> http://www.healthy.american.edu/nchf.html

6. The National Strength and Conditioning Association (NSCA)
Strength and conditioning specialists may wish to become affiliated with the National Strength and Conditioning Association. The NSCA is a nonprofit organization chartered in 1978 as an international authority on improving physical performance. Their address is:

> http://www.colosoft.com/nsca

7. National Federation of Professional Trainers (NFPT)
The NFPT also offers internationally recognized certification in weight training, educational information, magazines, and other resources. They are located at:

> http://www.nfpt.com/nfpt/

8. The Athletic Training Research and Education Society (ATRES)
This independent organization of personal trainers, educators, and allied health professionals serves to link research and education across the globe. The ATRES website also provides links to the physical education departments at Mankato State University, CSU (Chico), the University of Virginia, and other educational institutions.

> http://poe.acc.virginia.edu/~rjs5s/atres.html

9. The National Athletic Trainers Association (NATA)
The National Athletic Trainers Association, located in Dallas, Texas, is another important certifying organization. You can visit their site at:

http://www.nata.org/

Job searchers can benefit from NATA's "Careers in Athletic Training" site located at:

http://www.nata.org/careers/index.html

10. The American Chiropractic Association (ACA), which serves some 22,000 members, is a national spokes-organization for the chiropractic profession. You can browse their home page at:

http://www.cais.net/aca/aboutaca.htm

Detailed information about the profession is located at

http://www.cais.net/aca/chi-edu.htm

There are literally thousands of sites to choose from, but the "top 10" we've given here are a great place to start. You should, however, explore on your own. For instance, if you're interested in learning more about Jazzercise, the world's largest dance-fitness program, head to

http://www.jazzercise.com.

There's also the National Therapeutic Recreation Society, a branch of the National Recreation and Park Association. Its website is for persons interested in learning more about this interesting branch of rehabilitative medicine and can be found at

http://www.nrpa.org/

Aspiring therapists should also visit the on-line site of the American Physical Therapy Association. After visiting their home page at

http://www.apta.org/

you can see specific job descriptions such as their physical therapist site, which is at

http://www.apta.org/pt_prof/professionalprofile.html

and also their page for physical therapy assistants, at

http://www.apta.org/pt_prof/assistant.html.

The list of professional health fitness organizations in Appendix A furnishes additional Internet addresses. By the very nature of the World Wide Web, with new sites appearing each and every day, the list is by no means complete. It's up to you to turn on the search engine(s) of your choice and undertake the research necessary to learn more about this exciting field.

CHAPTER 6

CAREERS IN FITNESS INSTRUCTION

In this chapter we examine career opportunities on the fitness side of the health fitness constellation. This encompasses a wide and varied field. Fitness professionals may work as personal and athletic trainers, aerobic dance instructors, and school coaches. They may specialize in geriatrics, weight control, cardiac maintenance, or other areas. Others may work with all types of people.

GROUP-EXERCISE OR AEROBICS INSTRUCTOR

Group exercise is a term that encompasses all forms of exercise set to music. *Group-exercise instructors* lead group classes or give individual instruction. They demonstrate an exercise, explain its purpose, supervise clients to ensure that the exercise is being done correctly, set the pace, and determine the number and sequence of exercises. In many situations they also set the length of the class or program. The group-exercise instructor can choose to work full-time, part-time, or casually, as needed. Formats vary from beginning to advanced aerobics, Jazzercise, aquacize, stretch-and-tone, and prenatal/postpartum.

Another exciting area in this field is that of the *travel instructor.* Travel instructors teach vacationers on cruise ships. Others may fly to various cities or countries as a representative of their fitness organizations. Some may work at the fitness center of a luxury hotel or a summer health resort. Participants may be toddlers, teenagers, pre- or postnatal women, fifty-plus, overweight, athletes, or dance instructors themselves. It is the instructor's responsibility to seek any additional educational preparation necessary to teach individuals who need special attention. Lacking the knowledge required to deal effectively with these various groups can lead to unnecessary injury to clients and possible lawsuits for the instructor. It is, therefore, foolish for any instructor to accept a position for which he or she is not fully prepared.

No matter which path of group exercise you take, you will need adequate training with a basic course in anatomy/physiology and CPR. You will need the knowledge of health appraisal techniques, risk factor identification, and submaximal exercise testing results to properly recommend an exercise program. In addition you should be able to demonstrate appropriate techniques in motivation, counseling, teaching, and behavior modification to promote lifestyle changes. If you plan to become an independent contractor, you should also have experience teaching and choreographing group exercise.

Certification

At present no agreement has been reached on an industry-wide certification program, although certification programs do exist. Until standardized certification is available, you need to investigate those programs that are offering training. Several nationally recognized certification organizations are profiled in Chapter 15,

"Some Professional Organization and Training Center Profiles." Many health facilities require that their exercise instructors be certified. In addition, any outfit that hires you should provide you with training that prepares you for its particular format.

Job Description

In a small organization such as an independent health club, community center, or private company, you will teach classes with music and routines that either you or the organization have designed. It may be your responsibility to update music or routines at designated intervals, or this may be a joint decision to be made with other instructors. In large franchise organizations such as Jazzercise and Richard Simmons, the organization will probably provide the music and choreography on a routine basis. You may also be required to do studio maintenance or act as a salesperson or receptionist. Make sure you find out if any other duties are included in your job description.

Your position in an organization determines certain obligations. If you are considered an employee, you may need to do more than just instruct your class. You may also need to sweep the floors and/or perform other needed functions. If you own your own business, you will probably be able to have someone else sweep the floors so that you will be able to concentrate on teaching exercise classes. Owning your own business is covered in Chapter 11.

As an independent contractor, you are self-employed and can teach as many classes as you desire, keeping in mind that you yourself should not overexercise. You should be providing your students a safe role model to follow. Your places of employment are unlimited. You may choose, for example, to teach exercise to employees of a large insurance firm in the company gym. Schools, nursing homes, dance studios, and houses of worship are all potential places of employment for the independent contractor.

Fitness centers are no longer found only in urban centers and country resorts. Many cruise lines hire exercise instructors to provide their passengers with the opportunity for a good workout. Travel instructors teach various classes each day to all ages and types of people. Your clients may be on a business trip or just seeking pleasure and relaxation. This is a highly competitive area. If you enjoy adventure, your fringe benefits may include working at exclusive spas or on cruise ships such as Princess, Carnival, or Royal Caribbean Cruise Lines. You may even be selected to travel to other countries to teach. Therefore, to be favorably considered, you need to apply for this type of position preferably after you have successfully taught group-exercise classes for some time.

What Does It Cost to Get Started?

Usually, in the smaller organization, it costs nothing to get started, although you may be required to purchase a uniform and pay for your training or certification. Training and certification costs vary greatly. If you wish to become connected with a large organization, you may have to pay a franchise fee as high as $2,000, which may include your uniform, cassettes, music, and training. You might also have to provide your own cassette player.

Chapter 15 and Appendix A list large and small organizations to contact that will provide you with the latest information on training and certification costs. These organizations also can offer you tips on how to get started. You may wish to follow the suggestions for Internet use given in Chapter 5 and search under the keywords *group exercise* and *aerobics*.

As an independent instructor, the *minimum* amount you will need to get started is $2,000. This covers promotional fliers, telephone bills, business cards, and teaching accessories such as mats, hand weights, and exercise bars, in addition to your own clothing, shoes, and music. You may also need to pay monthly rent on your studio. Independent instructors must research the copyright laws as pertains to the music that will be played during the class. Under normal circumstances, you may not duplicate cassette tapes, records, or compact discs without permission. Duplicating tapes, records, or compact discs you already own may involve a nominal fee to the record company. You should also be covered with professional liability insurance to protect you if someone in your class is injured. Contact the health fitness professional organizations and training centers and refer to the advertisements in health fitness magazines for insurance companies that offer professional liability to instructors. It is also recommended that you seek business and tax management advice before getting started.

Traveling instructors usually provide their own music because of the variety of classes they teach. The organization that hires you will probably expect you to buy your own exercise clothing and shoes.

Income

A group-exercise instructor working in a small organization may make an hourly wage of $20 to $40. Employees of large organizations can make a slightly higher hourly wage. In a franchise position, the average income could be as high as $25,000 per year for a part-time commitment.

The independent contractor can expect to earn from $20 to $50 per hour. Some clubs and studios pay a salary plus commission based on the number of students you bring into your class. You may also be in a position to establish your own fee for a class, taking into consideration your overhead (studio rental, music licensing fees, and so forth). An average charge for a class is from $15 to $30 an hour, depending upon student special needs. Refer to Chapter 11, "Owning Your Own Group-Exercise Business" for additional information.

The hourly wage for a travel instructor is approximately $20 to $50. Keep in mind, though, that all the fringe benefits such as travel, room, and board that are usually covered by the organization that hires you.

Additional Information

Aerobics and Fitness Association of America
15250 Ventura Boulevard, Suite 200
Sherman Oaks, CA 91403-3297

IDEA, The International Association of Fitness Professionals
6190 Cornerstone Court East, Suite 204
San Diego, CA 92121-3773

Jazzercise, Inc.
2808 Roosevelt Street
Carlsbad, CA 92008

CORPORATE FITNESS INSTRUCTOR

The concept of fitness is changing, and so is corporate America. Across the nation, corporate fitness programs are being developed to help employees keep healthy, active, and productive. More than 500 major companies and countless smaller ones offer some form of fitness program for their employees, and the number is growing. Most corporate programs today focus not only on physical fitness but on mental fitness as well and include programs that help employees expand into a positive fitness lifestyle. In most corporate programs, cardiovascular fitness classes, such as aerobics, walking, jogging, swimming, and cross-country skiing are popular offerings. From the corporate perspective, these classes help reduce the incidence of cardiovascular disease, with its astronomical costs to the company. The incidence of chronic back pain and repetitive stress injury are also diminished, as morale and team-spirit is increased. You can learn more about how to plan a fitness program for a corporation in Chapter 11, "Owning Your Own Group-Exercise Business."

Job Description

A corporate fitness instructor may work in a large or small business, government organization, or hospital providing individual and/or group programs for employees, based on specific needs. You may find that if you are hired in this position, you may work either in a company's meeting room or fitness center or teach the company's employees at a local gym. The instructor may work with the company's medical staff in preparing programs. Employees are provided with a comprehensive fitness and lifestyle assessment, education in lifestyle change, and exercise classes. In some situations, because the program is designed to meet the employee's needs, you will be involved in program planning as well.

Some firms provide their employees with training in motivation boosting, leadership, and CPR, which helps the company keep its costs down. If the company uses employee volunteers, they become actively involved in program planning and may lead fitness classes. Employees may pay yearly dues to support their fitness program. Participants get consistent reinforcement and the information necessary to make changes in lifestyle habits.

Many companies offer complete wellness programs such as stress reduction, smoking cessation, fitness testing, and nutritional evaluation, in addition to group exercise. Larger firms may have their own weight and exercise rooms. Taking this comprehensive approach to fitness not only enhances the employee's motivation to exercise, but allows the fitness instructor to screen employees for potential health risks.

Employers are looking for people with an exercise physiology background coupled with knowledge in fitness testing, nutrition, stress management, business management, and human relations. Job candidates also should be prepared to teach workshops on stretching as a preventative measure for back pain and repetitive stress injury. A fitness pro should be adept at communicating with others and dealing with the variety of reactions he or she is likely to encounter among the participants in the programs.

Education

A bachelor's degree in exercise physiology, physical education, or a related field along with professional certification is the minimum requirement. It is preferable that job candidates hold either a master's degree or be matriculated in a graduate program. Larger firms that offer tuition reimbursement programs to its employees may extend this benefit to the fitness director as well.

Income

As a corporate fitness instructor, you can expect to make $28,000 to $35,000 per year depending on education, experience, and the size of the company. The company must be experiencing profitable business conditions before a fitness director will be hired, so it is likely that most fitness director positions will be available with substantial, well-established companies. In many cases a company will hire an exercise instructor to lead classes several times a week and pay these instructors $25 to $50 per hour. For job information, contact the physical education department or career placement office of your local college.

Additional Information

Association for Worksite Health Promotion
    60 Revere Drive, Suite 500
    Northbrook, IL 60062

(Formerly the Association for Fitness in Business)

GROUP AND PERSONAL TRAINERS

As a *personal trainer* you may spend your winters on the French Riviera. Or, you might be the trainer for a Hollywood movie star. One-on-one instruction, though, requires more expertise than teaching an aerobics class. Even if you are qualified, you may find that personal training is not suited to your personality. One-on-one training takes more energy than teaching a class. You have to understand the strengths and weaknesses of your clients.

You also have to be more personally involved. A personal trainer spends several hours with each client doing a fitness assessment and taking a personal history. You would also take a medical history and request a doctor's consent, if necessary. In addition you should know about your client's daily diet, habits, and goals. You should check her or him for flexibility, strength, and stamina. You should ask the client, "What do you want to attain? Do you want to do aerobics? Do you want to stretch and tone? Do you want to build muscle? Do you want to lose your gut?" Make sure you know what your client wants. You may have to work around the schedule of a busy executive or celebrity. Your client may have physical limitations or injuries or need personalized prescriptions or monitoring. People who travel may want a personal trainer to come to their hotel to work with them. There are others who take their personal trainers with them to travel around the world so that they can keep up their exercise routine. Most personal trainers average three clients a day. Most trainers agree that you should start by working with one or two people you know to get a feel for the work and see whether you really like it.

Education

Education, training, and background of trainers vary widely. Some have formal education in physical education, while others have a master's degree in exercise physiology. There are trainers who have a background in dance and others in weight training. A medical background, such as nursing, is also a valuable tool for the personal trainer to have. The main focus of personal trainers should be to continue to take courses and attend seminars to update their knowledge in health fitness.

Personal trainers also should prepare for certification from one or more of the internationally recognized sports and fitness organizations. A poorly prepared trainer can cause more harm than good, and there is also the issue of liability, so anyone who makes his or her primary income from training should research professional liability possibilities. Recommended certifying organizations are listed at the end of this section.

What Does It Cost to Get Started?

Although you could try any of the techniques mentioned in this chapter on how to get started, such as advertising, many personal trainers agree that the best way to promote this business is word-of-mouth. For most trainers, scheduling the clients they have is a bigger problem than acquiring new ones. You should realize that travel time is costly and can divide your hourly salary in half. The first six months, your work may not be physically demanding, but mentally you're required to give more than you can imagine. But, if you are successful with these first clients, they will soon be promoting you better than you could promote yourself. Fortunately you don't need a mobile gym to offer a varied program. Trainers hold workouts in a variety of places, including clients' homes, offices, parks, and hotels.

Trainers also frequently negotiate to work at specific gyms or health clubs as independent contractors. Some clubs may require a percentage of the trainer's gross fee, while others simply require the trainer be a regular club member. As a trainer you may want to use a variety of equipment, but much of this is portable, and you will want to custom design the program you offer your client.

Income

You can make $35 to $100 per hour or more as a personal trainer. To make this salary, though, you should be able to answer your client's questions during a workout, or know where to find the answer quickly. A client pays a trainer for education and experience. Another consideration is that if you decide to charge $75 a session but few people in your market can pay that much, you may be better off charging $50 a session and having twice or three times as many clients.

Certification and Additional Information

American Fitness Association
P.O. Box 461
Durango, CO 81302

Canadian Association for Health, Physical Education, Recreation, and Dance
1600 James Naismith Drive
Gloucester, Ontario
K1B 5N4 Canada

IDEA, The International Association of Fitness Professionals
6190 Cornerstone Court East, Suite 204
San Diego, CA 92121-3773

National Athletic Trainer's Association
2952 Stemmons Freeway
Dallas, TX 75247

National Federation of Professional Trainers
P.O. Box 4579
Lafayette, IN 47903-4579

National Strength and Conditioning Association
   P.O. Box 38909
   Colorado Springs, CO 80937

NAUTILUS INSTRUCTOR

At one time, weight equipment was found primarily in body-builder's gyms and YMCAs. Today, the concept of weight training has become so popular that you will find some form of equipment in almost any fitness facility or gym you visit. Until the mid-1950s, training to enhance muscle strength and endurance was done almost exclusively by lifting barbells and dumbbells. Later, specialized exercise machines appeared, which produced far more thorough training effects. The exercise machines quickly gained in popularity and have become the most widely used form of weight training by professional athletes and fitness enthusiasts. Most health and training clubs have a separate area of machines and free weights and are continually adding more people to their staffs who are trained specifically to counsel in machine and free weight exercise. The *weight training instructor* may be one of the most important positions in the facility due to the great risk of injury of an individual who is unfamiliar with the equipment. The weight training instructor counsels each user and observes progress carefully to instruct on improvement and safe applications of the equipment.

Job Description

An instructor in the use of free weights, standard resistance machines, or variable resistance equipment, should have an understanding of two things: the human body and the facility's weight equipment. An instructor should be able to answer questions and help club members with their workout. He or she is responsible for establishing a program for individuals interested in bodybuilding. The training instructor also must be able to advise on the amount of weight each person should begin with, and at what increments that person should increase his or her load.

Education

As with the personal trainer, a bachelor's degree in exercise physiology is a good start; so is the training provided by the equipment manufacturer. Nautilus programs, for example, provide a high level of instruction for those who will be working in facilities that feature Nautilus equipment.

Income

A weight trainer whose background includes only on-the-job training may be working at a little above minimum wage, whereas the trainer with a formal education background and extensive experience can expect to make up to $50 per hour depending upon the place of employment. For additional information, contact the organizations listed earlier in the *personal trainer* section of this chapter.

EXERCISE PHYSIOLOGIST

Exercise physiology is the science that deals with the study of muscular activity and the associated functional responses and adaptations. Therefore, an exercise physiologist is interested in the influence of exercise on these body functions. An exercise physiologist must have a general understanding of the scientific bases underlying the exercise-induced physiological responses. He or she is an independent research scientist who has earned a doctoral degree with an emphasis in the life sciences and has a primary research interest in physical exercise.

Job Description

Exercise physiologists conduct controlled investigations of responses and adaptations to muscular activity utilizing subjects in a clinical setting, a research institute, or an academic institution. In addition they often teach academic courses in exercise physiology, environmental physiology, or applied human physiology for students of medicine, physiology, physical education, and other health-related fields. Some work at YMCAs, JCCs, and other community centers or in commerce and industry, rehabilitation programs, and competitive sports programs.

Education

If you are interested in working toward a Ph.D., which is necessary for research and/or teaching, opportunities for graduate study are available within academic programs of medicine, physiology, biology, physical education, kinesiology, exercise science, and biochemistry at many universities.

To work in the commercial/industrial area, you would need a degree from the department of physical education, exercise science, or health science and nutrition. Any health-related setting that employs exercise physiologists will require a degree in health science, physical therapy, physical education, kinesiology, or exercise science.

The undergraduate curriculum is influenced by an individual's career choice. Preparation in general biology, chemistry, biochemistry, physics, mathematics, and computer science is important if a research and teaching career is desired. In some professional programs, the curriculum is well defined. For some employment opportunities, valuable training in specific areas more directly applicable can be selected by the undergraduate student.

Students interested in exercise physiology should visit the various types of employment settings to gain further insight concerning the necessary training and background, the certification prerequisites, the job responsibility, the general work environment, and the employment potential.

Income

Exercise physiologists encounter a broad range of wages and salaries. Depending upon the amount of education and the place of employment, wages can vary from $15 to more than $50 an hour. Academic positions are offered as postdoctoral fellowships and assistant professorships, and range from $28,000 to $40,000 for entry-level positions.

YOGA INSTRUCTOR

Relaxation is as important to good health as exercise because it relieves tension. Yoga is an exercise system, formulated in the *ashrams* (places where people meet for spiritual instruction) of India centuries ago, that takes the entire human being into account more naturally than almost any other training system. Because the mind, body, and spirit interconnect, yoga teaches how to sustain yourself in peace and comfort throughout life. Yoga is a form of disciplined practice that promotes mental and physical well-being through physical postures called *asanas,* which are performed in correlation with proper breathing technique. Studies have shown that the relaxation posture effectively reduces high blood pressure. Many physicians now recommend yoga to combat back ailments, sleeping disorders, and other stress-related problems. It is an excellent technique to aid an individual's mental well-being.

Integrating yoga postures and principles into your schedule can add dimensions of flexibility, stamina, breathing control, relaxation, and mental astuteness that will inject new life into your aerobics and strength workouts. Instructors are employed by small and large organizations, including schools, health clubs, churches, and private homes.

Job Description

A *yoga instructor* has usually studied and trained under the direction of another yoga instructor. Instructors are responsible for leading a class through asanas and, in some situations, meditation as well. Although the postures look simple, they can be quite difficult for a beginner. It can take about ten weeks to teach a person how to relax quickly and deeply. Instructors assess individual students for proper body alignment and breathing technique. Some instructors also teach nutrition classes, and others work with special-needs groups such as the disabled, elderly, and HIV-positive. Yoga instructors may have been educated through courses in an academic setting, attending seminars, or self-study.

Personal Qualifications

Qualifications should include emotional stability, patience, and a calm, warm personality. Yoga instructors should possess the ability to "choreograph" their asanas in a smooth flowing manner so that the client is completely relaxed at the end of the session. An instructor should be able to choose music that is soothing and calming for the participants.

Education

Study and practice under the direction of a yoga instructor is usually all that is required to qualify you to teach yoga, although it is advisable to check on teaching certification in any given locality. Although it is not mandatory, a teaching certificate indicates that serious time and interest have been invested in the subject. To gain a further edge in the market, aspiring yoga instructors should consider attending workshops in reflexology, nutrition, and exercise physiology.

Income

Instructors can expect to make approximately $20 to $30 per hour depending upon the size and type of organization that employs them. Many private instructors who teach in homes or studios make a substantially better income per session.

Additional Information

American Yoga Association
  513 South Orange Avenue
  Sarasota, FL 34236

International Yoga School (Correspondence Courses in Yoga and
    Reflexology)
    P.O. Box 23
    Torquay, Devon
    TQ2 8YE England
    E-mail: courses@theiys.demon.co.uk

Don't forget to browse the Yoga website on the Internet's
"Yahoo!" engine at:

    http://www.yahoo.com/Society_and_Culture/Religion/Yoga/

CHAPTER 7

CAREERS IN HEALTH FITNESS MEDICINE

The career opportunities discussed in this chapter concern health fitness medicine. They require many years of study, so commitment, educational background and aspirations, personal finances, age, and logistics will be factors in your decision to enter this branch of health fitness. You can find more detailed information about these careers in *Opportunities in Health and Medical Careers.* If you are interested in additional careers associated with health fitness, refer to other VGM Career Horizons books, such as *Opportunities in Sports and Athletics* and *Opportunities in Sports Medicine.*

OSTEOPATHIC PHYSICIAN (D.O.)

Job Description

Osteopathic medicine is geared primary to the field of general practice. Presently, there are many opportunities for general practitioners.

Like M.D.s, osteopathic physicians, also called doctors of osteopathic medicine, are in fact licensed physicians but their focus is the body's musculoskeletal system. They use currently accepted methods of diagnosing and treating disease including dispensing medication and surgery. Osteopathic physicians also use osteopathic manipulation in diagnosis and treatment. High scholastic performance, integrity, initiative, an inquiring mind, sound judgment, and emotional stability are necessary for success in the field.

Osteopathic physicians work primarily in private practice; the majority of D.O.s are general practitioners. Other areas where they work include hospitals, research, teaching, military service, medical administration, the government, and public health.

Education

A minimum of three years of college working on a bachelor's degree and scoring competitively on the Medical College Admission Test (MCAT) are required for entrance into one of the colleges of osteopathic medicine. Most osteopathic colleges offer a four-year program with a few offering an accelerated three-year program. After completion of the program, the Doctor of Osteopathy (D.O.) degree is awarded and a twelve-month internship is then required. To further specialize, additional residencies are necessary; these last from one to five years. Once in practice, all D.O.s must complete at least 150 credit hours of continuing medical education.

Income

The salary of the osteopathic physician is comparable to that of the practicing M.D. Median income per year after expenses is currently $156,000.

Additional Information

American Osteopathic Association
142 East Ohio Street
Chicago, IL 60611

PHYSICIAN (M.D.)

Job Description

A physician is a professional who has been trained to care for the health and well-being of people. The care is preventive or restorative in nature and may be centered around the whole person, as in the case of a general practitioner, or specific parts or systems of the body, as in the case of a cardiologist or endocrinologist. There are many subfields of medicine in which a physician can specialize after completing her or his general training. A person who desires to be a physician should have emotional stability, intelligence, sound judgment, ability to make difficult decisions, good interpersonal skills, and compassion for others.

The majority of physicians are self-employed, but some work in institutional medicine, research or technology, administration, government agencies, public health, or the military. Many physicians in the fitness field work in the area of sports medicine. A *sports orthopedic surgeon,* for example, diagnoses and treats bone and muscle injuries and works with patients to develop a fitness program designed to avoid future injuries.

Education

Four years of college with courses in biology, chemistry, and other sciences, and scoring competitively on the Medical College Admissions Test (MCAT) are needed to gain admission to an accredited college of medicine. Depending upon the curriculum, three or four years of study in medical school are in most cases followed by at least one to three years as a resident in a postgraduate-based program. To specialize in other areas of medicine, one to six years of postgraduate education may be taken in the area of specialization.

Income

After accounting for the costs of establishing and maintaining a practice, including professional liability insurance, net earnings for general practitioners average between $110,000 and $150,000. Earnings for specialists such as anesthesiologists exceed $200,000 per year. Note that geography and managed care can greatly impact earnings.

Additional Information

Council on Medical Education
   American Medical Association
   515 North State Street
   Chicago, IL 60610

Pre-med students with aspirations in health fitness may also wish to contact the following:

American College of Sports Medicine
   P.O. Box 1440
   One Virginia Avenue
   Indianapolis, IN 46206

American Orthopaedic Society for Sports Medicine
70 West Hubbard
Chicago, IL 60610

DOCTOR OF CHIROPRACTIC (D.C.)

Job Description

Doctors of chiropractic, also known as *chiropractic physicians* or simply *chiropractors,* diagnose and treat patients whose health problems are associated with the musculoskeletal and nervous systems, especially the spine. The theory behind chiropractic holds that spinal or vertebral dysfunction, called a "subluxation," alters many important body functions by affecting the nervous system. Chiropractors follow a standard routine to secure the information needed for diagnosis and treatment. They take the patient's medical history, conduct physical, neurological, and orthopedic examinations, and may order or perform X-ray or other diagnostic imaging. Unlike physicians, chiropractors rely on neither medications nor invasive procedures.

Most chiropractors work in solo practice or in partnerships. They must possess keen observation skills and also considerable hand dexterity to perform manipulations. As with other health-care providers, they should be empathic, understanding, and have the desire to help and teach others.

Education

At least two years of undergraduate education are required to gain admission to chiropractic school, although a four-year degree with extensive course work in physiology, biology, and biochemistry is recommended. The professional program is four years, after which the candidate must successfully pass all or part of the three-part test administered by the National Board of Chiropractic Examiners. Some states may require additional examinations before licensure is granted.

Income

Chiropractors in solo practice average a net income of approximately $75,000. The highest 10 percent earned above $150,000 in 1995. The field is becoming more competitive, although the number of chiropractors maintaining full-time practices is expected to grow faster than the average for all occupations through the year 2005.

Additional Information

American Chiropractic Association
  1701 Claredon Boulevard
  Arlington, VA 22209

International Chiropractors Association
  1110 North Glebe Road, Suite 1000
  Arlington, VA 22201

World Chiropractic Alliance
  2950 North Dobson Road, Suite 1
  Chandler, AZ 85224-1802

For a listing of U.S. chiropractic colleges, contact:

Council on Chiropractic Education
  7975 North Hayden Road, Suite A-210
  Scottsdale, AZ 85258

CHAPTER 8

CAREERS IN HEALTH FITNESS REHABILITATION

In this chapter we will examine the health fitness opportunities that involve helping people in clinical settings by employing other noninvasive techniques. This broad spectrum of opportunities mostly involves one or another dimension of rehabilitation therapy. Some patients will attain 100 percent restoration of movement and other skills, while others will be taught to adjust to living a full and content life with physical or other impairments. Some patients will be taught how to make themselves as comfortable as possible. A small percentage of therapists will work with professional athletes dedicated to optimizing their performance by adding a certified health-care professional to their training team.

DANCE/MOVEMENT THERAPIST

The *dance/movement therapist* uses movement in the treatment and rehabilitation of children and adults with neurological or other physical impairments and/or social, emotional, or cognitive challenges. This work is distinguished from other types of dance by its focus on the nonverbal aspects of behavior and its use of movement. A dance/movement therapist, also referred to simply as a *dance therapist,* works with people who require special psycho-therapeutic services because of behavioral, learning, perceptual, and/or physical disorders. The therapist uses knowledge of how the body moves in relation to space and rhythm, which helps a person develop coordination, improve gait, and correct problems in mobility. The emotionally impaired are assisted by the dance therapist's observations, which aid in the development of a behavior modification program utilizing dance and music.

Job Description

Skilled dance/movement therapists must be well trained in the art of dance and well versed in psychopathology and human development. Dance/movement therapists are employed in psychiatric hospitals, clinics, day treatment programs, community mental health centers, developmental centers, correctional facilities, special schools, and rehabilitation facilities. He or she works with people of all ages and in all socioeconomic levels, both in group and individual situations. Job opportunities for trained professionals vary in different locations. Many dance/movement therapists are pioneering job development in their region, and the American Dance Therapy Association has, since its inception in 1966, strived to enhance job opportunities for dance/movement therapists.

Education

A bachelor's or master's degree in special education, kinesiology, psychology, or a related field may be sufficient if the person's dance background is very strong and if he or she has additional dance therapy training and a supervised clinical internship. The American Dance Therapy Association recommends that students preparing for a career as a dance/movement therapist first obtain a broad liberal arts background with an emphasis in psychology, in addition to extensive training in a wide variety of dance forms. Students should also study choreography and kinesiology.

Professional training is concentrated at the master's level. Studies include courses such as dance/movement therapy theory and practice, human development, observation and research skills, and a supervised internship in a clinical setting. Candidates may apply for certification as a DTR (Dance Therapist Registered), which qualifies master's degree recipients to work in a professional treatment system. Candidates may also apply for the ADTR distinction (Academy of Dance Therapists Registered), which demonstrates additional requirements have been met qualifying the recipient to teach, provide supervision, and engage in private practice.

Additional Information

American Dance Therapy Association
  2000 Century Plaza, Suite 108
  1063 Little Patuxent Parkway
  Columbia, MD 21044-3263

OCCUPATIONAL THERAPIST

Job Description

Occupational therapists work with persons who have experienced physical injuries or illnesses, sensory or tactile deficiencies, psychological or developmental disorders, or problems and impediments associated with the aging process. The occupational therapist coordinates a variety of educational, vocational, and rehabilitation therapies to allow the patient to become as self-sufficient as possible and lead as normal a life as possible in work, education, and pleasure. Tact, creativity, ability to solve complex living problems, and an interest in helping others are necessary. Occupational therapists work in hospitals, clinics, extended care facilities, rehabilitation hospitals, government agencies, and community agencies.

Education

Four years of college with a major in occupational therapy is the training required to become an occupational therapist. Thirty-nine states, Puerto Rico, and the District of Columbia require occupational therapists to obtain a license to practice. Applicants must have a degree or post-undergraduate certification from an accredited school before they can sit for the National Certification Examination, which is required to become a registered occupational therapist. A master's degree or a certificate program can be taken for those who already have an undergraduate degree in occupational therapy.

Income

An occupational therapist earns from $33,700 to $50,000 a year, on average. The ratio of job positions to the number of qualified professionals is positive and will only increase in the next ten years. Ethnic, cultural, and linguistic diversity is especially needed in this growing field.

Additional Information

American Occupational Therapy Association
  4720 Montgomery Lane
  Bethesda, MD 20814-3425

Canadian Association of Occupational Therapists
  110 Eglinton Avenue West
  Toronto, Ontario
  M4R 1A3 Canada

OCCUPATIONAL THERAPY ASSISTANT

Job Description

An *occupational therapy assistant* helps the occupational therapist conduct a series of educational, vocational, and rehabilitation activities aimed at enabling disabled individuals to reach their highest functional levels possible. An occupational therapy assistant works under the supervision of a registered occupational therapist and assists by preparing materials for activities, maintaining tools and equipment, and recording and reporting on a patient's progress. They may help teach patients to manipulate wheelchairs or to stretch and make limber certain muscles. Persons who seek employment as occupational therapy assistants should have a desire to help others and display understanding, tact, and patience when working with the disabled. Occupational therapy assistants work in hospitals, nursing homes, rehabilitation centers, psychiatric hospitals, and military and veterans hospitals.

Education

Preparation for a career as an occupational therapy assistant can be achieved through a two-year associate degree program, through a one-year program at an accredited institution, or through a twenty-five-week program conducted in a hospital setting.

Income

Occupational therapy assistants can earn approximately $25,000 to $30,000 a year, depending upon experience, education, and geographical location.

OCCUPATIONAL THERAPY AIDE

An *occupational therapy aide* assists the occupational therapist by preparing materials and equipment for use during patient treatment. An occupational therapy aide may also provide a range of clerical or other tasks such as scheduling appointments, restocking or ordering supplies, and filling out insurance forms. No formal education beyond a high school diploma is required, but applicants should possess strong interpersonal skills and a desire to help people in need.

Income

Jobs for occupational therapy aides are often part-time positions, with salaries starting between $6.00 and $7.00 per hour.

Starting salaries tend to be higher in privately owned practices and nursing homes than in hospitals.

PHYSICAL THERAPIST

A *physical therapist,* known in Canada and the United Kingdom as a *physiotherapist,* plans and administers physical therapy treatment programs for patients to restore or improve function, relieve pain, and prevent disability following disease, injury, or surgical amputation. Physical therapists use the treatment modalities of electricity, heat, cold, ultrasound, massage, and exercise. He or she also helps the patient to mentally or emotionally accept her or his disability and begin the healing process by encouraging development. Responsibility, sincerity, and emotional stability are assets in seeking a career in physical therapy.

Physical therapists work in hospitals, outpatient clinics, rehabilitation centers, home care agencies, nursing homes, voluntary health agencies, private practices, sports medicine centers, educational systems, and in clinical research activities. Physical therapists also work with athletes striving to achieve their maximum physical abilities through training under medical supervision. Today's physical therapist is as much a teacher and educator as a rehabilitation clinician.

Education

A four-year degree with extensive courses in the humanities, English, writing, psychology, biology, chemistry, physics, and statistics is the first step toward becoming a physical therapist. It is becoming the norm for aspirants to pursue a master's degree in physical therapy for professional credentialing owing to the industry's every-growing standards.

After graduating from an accredited degree program, candidates must pass a state-administered national examination. Additional requirements vary from state to state and can be obtained by contacting state boards directly. Physical therapists may choose to become certified by the American Board of Physical Therapy Specialties in any of seven following areas: cardiopulmonary, clinical electrophysiology, geriatrics, neurology, orthopedics, pediatrics, and sports physical therapy. Eligibility for certification is achieved only after several years of clinical experience.

Income

In 1995 there were approximately 90,000 registered physical therapists in the United States. Median salaries were $37,600, with the nation's top 10 percent earning $61,700 and the bottom 10 percent earning less than $20,000. Therapists in private and group practices earned slightly higher than the national medians. The job outlook is positive, especially for therapists in solo and group practice and for those with experience in multicultural and bilingual environments.

Additional Information

American Physical Therapy Association
    1111 North Fairfax Street
    Alexandria, VA 22314

(Enclose SASE for the APTA's bulletin, *A Future in Physical Therapy.*)

PHYSICAL THERAPIST ASSISTANT
Job Description

A *physical therapist assistant, physical therapy assistant,* or *PTA,* is a skilled health-care provider who works under the direction of the physical therapist in the treatment of the patient. The assistant follows the patient care program devised by the physical therapist and physician by performing test and treatment procedures, assembling equipment necessary for procedures, and observing and reporting on patients' behavior. Maturity, patience, and a desire to help people are assets in this position. Physical therapist assistants practice in hospitals, nursing homes, rehabilitation centers, and community and government agencies.

Education

Training for a physical therapist assistant career is a two-year associate degree program. More than half of all states require physical therapist assistants to be licensed, registered, or certified. Physical therapist assistants should be certified in CPR and first aid.

Income

Salaries for recent graduates range from $18,000 to $25,000, while the median income after five to ten years in the field is

$30,000, a substantial increase over the salaries reported in the 1991 edition of this book.

PHYSICAL THERAPY AIDE

Job Description

The role of the *physical therapy aide* is to assist the physical therapist in patient care. The responsibilities include preparing and maintaining treatment areas, assisting patients in preparation for treatment, and carrying out exercise and ambulation programs as assigned or supervised by the physical therapist. An interest in working with people, the ability to communicate, and a pleasant personality are assets in this position. Physical therapy aides work in hospitals, rehabilitation centers, nursing homes, military and veterans hospitals, and psychiatric hospitals.

Education

A high school diploma or the equivalent is required for working in this position. Physical therapy aides should be certified in CPR and first aid.

Income

Salaries for physical therapy aides average about $22,500.

REHABILITATION/THERAPEUTIC RECREATION THERAPIST

Rehabilitation therapists and *therapeutic recreation therapists* usually direct both indoor and outdoor activities. They may perform a great deal of physical exercise while conducting sports and dance programs. These specialists are employed in hospitals, rehabilitation centers, schools offering special education programs, nursing homes, correctional institutions, and homes for the aged.

Job Description

Rehabilitation therapists are responsible for conducting, organizing, and administering recreation and leisure programs designed to aid in the recovery or improve the adjustment of persons who are ill, physically or mentally challenged, or behaviorally disturbed. They organize both individual and group activities for children as well as adults. Therapists often work with other professionals, including physicians, psychologists, psychiatrists, nurses, and teachers. They determine the needs of the individuals or groups and may recommend programs involving exercise, social participation, group interaction, or hobbies to meet the desired objectives. Therapists encourage individuals to participate in the selected activities and offer assistance, instruction, and leadership when necessary. They observe the individuals during the program and prepare reports to aid in evaluating their social, mental, or physical progress. These reports will then be used by other members of the health care team in coordinating patient care.

Therapists employed by rehabilitation institutions may consult with individuals who are being discharged, advising them of recreation programs and facilities in their communities and then arranging for their participation in these programs. Additional responsibilities of rehabilitation therapists may include hiring, training, and supervising both volunteer and paid recreation workers. They may also prepare and submit program budgets, order equipment and supplies, maintain accurate financial and personnel records, and analyze and make recommendations for improving the recreation program. In addition they may be responsible for scheduling and supervising the use of all equipment and facilities.

Personal Attributes

Good physical health, stamina, a pleasant personality, and a sincere desire to help people are necessary for a career as a recreational therapist. You should have an interest in working with people of all ages and backgrounds and be able to inspire confidence in their capabilities. In addition you should possess a keen sense of humor, patience, ingenuity, creative imagination, and the ability to express yourself clearly, be it orally, physically with the use of body language, or in writing. You will be a mentor and clinician for a wide gamut of people, from traumatized children to lonely and frightened seniors to accident survivors to patients devastated by AIDS.

Education

Rehabilitation therapists should have an extensive knowledge of functional anatomy, exercise physiology, pathology, electrocardiography, human behavior/psychology, and gerontology as well as knowledge of the principles and practices of graded exercise testing, exercise prescription, exercise leadership skills, and emergency procedures. Courses in these disciplines are available at the undergraduate and graduate levels.

During high school, aspirants to this career should complete a college entrance program. It is important to include courses in public speaking, art, and music. Participation in as many sport and athletic activities as possible also is recommended.

Although an associate degree in recreational therapy from an accredited junior college or community college will qualify aspirants for jobs requiring far less specialized skills, completion of at least a bachelor's degree in recreation with an emphasis in rehabilitation or therapeutic recreation is recommended. Certification also should be sought as early as possible. Beginning with an associate degree may be a good route toward getting a job temporarily, while you continue schooling on a part-time basis. It can also serve the purpose of providing experience with work in the field to allow you to test your interest and commitment in this area. Therapeutic recreation therapists with graduate degrees and a substantial number of clinical hours may apply for the title of CTRS, Certified Therapeutic Recreation Specialist, through the National Therapeutic Recreation Society.

Income

Incomes vary according to size, type, and geographical location of the organization, and education and experience of the individual. Average earnings for recreation therapists in the federal government were slightly above $30,000 in 1991 and $35,954 in 1995, indicating growth in the field. Nursing home compensation was lower, in the area of $17,000 to $25,000, while total average salaries at the time of this writing were around $32,000. There are approximately 35,000 recreational therapists currently employed in the United States. The outlook is positive, particularly in community residential facilities as well as day treatment programs for people with disabilities.

Additional Information

American Therapeutic Recreation Association
P.O. Box 15215
Hattiesburg, MS 39402-5215

National Council for Therapeutic Recreation Certification
P.O. Box 479
Thiells, NY 10984-0479

National Therapeutic Recreation Society
2775 South Quincy Street, Suite 300
Arlington, VA 22206-2204

KINESIOLOGY AND OTHER OPPORTUNITIES

We have already seen that there are many other opportunities that fall under the umbrella of health fitness. Kinesiology, a diverse field having to do with body mechanics, offers a multitude of possibilities. Some physical therapists specialize in this branch of therapy. Graduates with degrees in kinesiology also can work as consultants to industries that make sporting equipment and attire, especially running shoes. Others go on to become rehabilitation or physical therapists themselves. Still others earn Ph.D.s and research and teach in the field.

Nursing, nutrition, nurse-midwifery, hand therapy, park rangers, orthotics and prosthetics, among others, are all viable opportunities in this rich and diverse field. Professionals in these areas work directly with patients in hospital settings, at home, and at play. Nurse-midwives, for example, require special training since they must undertake invasive procedures. Hand therapists are physical or occupational therapists who work exclusively with patients suffering impairments due to birth defects, accident or injury, age, arthritis, or repetitive strain syndrome owing to misuse of equipment at home or at the workplace. Certified orthotists (COs) and certified prosthetists (CPs) make and fit artificial limbs or devices to enable better use of damaged limbs. Descriptions of these and other careers can be found in specialized books in VGM's *Opportunities* series. Therapists are also needed to work in an area seldom talked about: to help victims of torture cope with the physical and psychological injuries inflicted upon them by repressive regimes. These people perhaps need the greatest physical and psychological care, as "doctors" are often present when the injuries are being inflicted.

CHAPTER 9

THE HEALTH CLUB

A health club is a multifaceted fitness facility that, either by itself or as part of a larger chain operation, usually operates on a profit-making basis. The earliest health clubs were substantially different from today's clubs and identified themselves as health spas. Their focus was on relaxation features such as whirlpools, steam rooms, and body massage.

Today's health clubs emphasize exercise rather than relaxation and provide a wealth of equipment, services, and fitness systems for their members to use. Many health clubs also provide clients with opportunities for swimming, running, stretching, and weight training. A full service health club also features aerobic conditioning equipment, exercise classes, and a spa area. Most upscale clubs also have tennis and racquetball courts.

Many of the careers discussed in this chapter are also open to those not working in a health club.

HEALTH CLUB ADMINISTRATIVE PERSONNEL

The administrative members of the club include managers, salespeople, and others who are concerned with the business side of the operation. An efficient staff can provide its members with a cost-effective, well-run facility. If the administration is weak, the club will probably have low standards and be disorganized, so examine the club carefully before you accept a job. Salaries in these areas are dependent upon club size and your education and experience.

Desk Receptionist

The desk receptionist is the first person that members and prospective members meet when they enter a facility. This person is the facility's public relations person, and the degree of friendliness and helpfulness you find here is representative of the facility as a whole. The receptionist's chief responsibility is to control the flow of traffic into the club and to answer the telephones. The receptionist also welcomes new members, provides them with basic information, and introduces them to a salesperson who will give them a tour and description of the programs available. The desk receptionist also may have responsibility for security, as the receptionist is the person who usually checks membership ID cards.

Salesperson

The chief duty of the salesperson is to sell club memberships. Salespersons tour the facility with prospective members and encourage membership. If the person does not immediately join, the salesperson may follow up with mailings and phone calls. They often rely on commissions for their incomes, and weekly reports keep their employers informed about productivity.

Manager/Assistant Manager

A manager's responsibility is to coordinate the efforts of all administrative, fitness, and auxiliary personnel. The manager sets the tone for the entire club, and the quality of the facility is a reflection of the manager's concern and expertise. This is probably the most stressful position in a health club as the manager/assistant manager deals constantly with both the staff and the public.

HEALTH CLUB FITNESS PERSONNEL

Exercise Program Director

The *exercise program director* heads the fitness staff. This key person must have a number of attributes in addition to a personal commitment to physical fitness. These skills include managing, testing, and communicating. The ability to plan, implement, and evaluate programs is critical. Exercise program directors design, implement, and administer safe, effective, and enjoyable preventive and rehabilitative exercise programs. They are responsible for seeing that class instructors and supervisors deliver a competent, consistent level of service. Therefore, they train their staffs, instilling the required knowledge, competencies, and skills necessary for administration of these tests and activities. The director educates and communicates with members of the community about exercise programs. A qualified director usually has a background oriented more toward exercise than business. The director may have a degree in physical education or exercise physiology, certification in sports medicine, or training in another related area. For additional information see the section on exercise physiologist in Chapter 6. More information also can be found in VGM Career

Horizon's *Opportunities in Sports Medicine* and *Opportunities in Physical Therapy Careers.*

Exercise Test Technologist

This is a layperson with training in how to test the following: standing height, weight, resting heart rate, resting blood pressure, and body composition. Technologists administer, under appropriate direction, graded exercise testing procedures consistent with the individual's age and health status and record data collected before, during, and after the graded exercise test. If necessary they are able to implement emergency procedures and thus need current certification in cardiopulmonary resuscitation (CPR).

Consultant

The consultant may be an individual, such as a physician who specializes in sports medicine, or a firm that advises on physical testing and profiling. A good consultant is usually someone who does not represent specific manufacturers within the fitness industry; instead, this individual has a broad interest and background in overall development of fitness programs. If you are interested in the health fitness aspect of medicine, you can find more information in two other books in the VGM Career Horizons series, *Opportunities in Health and Medical Careers* and *Opportunities in Sports Medicine.*

Martial Arts Instructor

The *martial arts* encompass many forms of study and practice such as *karate, tai chi, judo, aikido,* and *tae kwon do,* to name a few. Each area has its own requirements in order to earn *belts* and/ or *degrees* that would enable one to become an instructor. The teaching of self-defense has become a very popular addition to many clubs, and the training requirements for instructors are stringent, due largely to the potential for injury in these strenuous physical activities.

Each discipline in this group requires a specific progression of skill development to reach each level of recognition. If you are interested in the martial arts, you should discuss your training program with well-recognized instructors in your area and plan to work for several different organizations to see if you enjoy this type of employment.

Lifeguard

The *lifeguard*'s chief function is to coordinate and control pool traffic, maintaining safety for all in the pool and its immediate environment. Lifeguards are also responsible for checking the temperature and quality of the pool's water several times a day. In many facilities, the lifeguard is also required to teach swimming classes, often to people of various ages and abilities. Standards require lifeguards to hold certificates in a lifesaving program, such as that offered by the Red Cross.

Racquet Sports Instructor

This position is often held by someone who is an accomplished player of the racquet sports. University training and certification is usually not necessary, although well-known players may receive preference in hiring, especially in fashionable, expensive clubs.

Diet Counselor

Health spas and upscale clubs may retain diet counselors with various backgrounds. Some may just be well versed on diet and nutrition from studying on their own. Other may have a more extensive background. A *dietician* receives formal training at a university or nursing school and is registered or certified. A *nutritionist* is a person who has studied nutrition, either at a university or nursing school, and is registered or certified. To learn more about dieticians and nutritionists, refer to *Opportunities in Nutrition Careers,* a VGM Career Horizons book.

Masseur and Masseuse

A good *masseur* or *masseuse* should have a thorough understanding of anatomy and physiology. Masseurs have usually studied massage in a school or acted as apprentices to licensed instructors. Some specialize in giving only facial message; others are trained in Swedish massage, use of hydrotherapy, and other specialties. Licenses and certification are required in many states. You should inquire at your local licensing and certification department to find out the requirements in your area.

Spa and Locker Room Attendant

There are usually no requirements or experience necessary to become a *spa or locker room attendant.* Although the work will vary a great deal in different locales, some basic duties can be expected in most places. The attendant is responsible for seeing that the locker room and spa areas are clean and usable throughout the day. The attendant may also dispense toiletries, provide security to the area, and assist patrons as needed. This is an excellent job for the beginner who wants to learn about fitness careers. It is often possible to get a part-time job or a seasonal job so you can see where your interests lie.

Nursery Attendant

A *nursery attendant* usually does not hold a degree or certification in the area of child development. This is a person who enjoys children and keeps them clean, fed, and cared for while their parents are participating at the club. This is another good job for a person who wants to learn about the inside operations of a fitness center, spa, or health club. If you are interested in such a job for the summer, it is a good idea to apply to the director of the club several months in advance.

CHAPTER 10

SPECIAL PROGRAMS FOR SPECIAL PEOPLE

PRE- OR POSTNATAL

A woman does not need to stop exercising if she becomes pregnant. Actually, a woman has a better labor and delivery if she is physically fit. Professionally supervised exercise is one of the best conditioning methods for pregnant women.

Prenatal (before delivery) and postnatal or postpartum (after delivery) programs are now recognized as being important to the well-being of women. Many physicians now recommend exercise programs for their patients. There are even some physicians who refuse to accept patients unless they are in exercise programs!

Many programs have developed across the country for this type of client. For prenatal exercise programs, the need for proper supervision is extremely important, for the woman as well as her unborn child.

To quote Dr. Steven Van Camp, "The purpose of prenatal programs are two-fold. Not only do prenatal programs provide an environment of activity tailored to the expectant mother, but also a safe, supportive situation where she can share her feelings with women experiencing the same physical and emotional changes. She need not feel out of place while exercising and, indeed, she can gain a sense of self and increased excitement about her delivery."

The instructor of this type of client should be extremely sensitive to the needs of the participants. You should allow time before or after class to discuss the needs of your clients. Before each session, you should tell clients to let you know when they have any physical discomfort during the exercise session. You need to be particularly aware during the time you are teaching of anyone becoming dizzy or pale, nauseated, experiencing breathing difficulties, or having excessive fatigue.

Ellyn Lederman Novick and Debra Grant, both registered nurses and certified (Lamaze) childbirth educators, have combined their prenatal experience with dance-exercise programs. Both nurses worked in a maternity center and in a newborn care unit for premature babies before starting a fitness program at the Childbirth Education and Fitness Center in Connecticut.

Ellyn and Debra discovered that many women wanted more than the Lamaze classes they were teaching. They continued to teach Lamaze because they felt the techniques helped couples cope with labor and delivery, in addition to helping the father understand his role as coach. In addition, though, they decided to offer a more comprehensive program that included pre- and postnatal as well as infant/parent exercise and massage.

Ellyn and Debra's classes are specifically designed to develop and tone the muscles during pregnancy and delivery. These exercises incorporate Lamaze breathing techniques, proper body alignment, and relaxation/concentration methods. Students attending their class also receive a workbook outlining the benefits of a fitness program and special considerations while exercising. They do not categorize their exercises as "aerobic." There are many physicians today who believe that aerobics during pregnancy diminishes the blood flow to the developing fetus. This could prove especially dangerous to the woman who has not been exercising before she became pregnant. Debra suggests that a woman who has not been exercising regularly should not start their class until after the twelfth week of pregnancy.

Ellyn and Debra spent a summer going to nearly every obstetrician in Greenwich and Westport, Connecticut, to explain their program. Now they get most of their students through referrals by obstetricians. They also believed an advisory board was important, and their advisers include an obstetrician, internist, dentist, neonatal nurse clinician, and a pediatrician. They also require a note from each participant's primary care physician before she can begin classes.

Both Ellyn and Debra carry malpractice insurance as a legal precaution. In starting your own business, you should clarify your legal liabilities, those of your students, and the building or facility you occupy.

OLDER/OVERWEIGHT/OUT-OF-SHAPE

The best thing you can do with over-fifty, overweight, out-of-shape students is to keep encouraging them and slow down your routines. You can teach them about exercise and how to stay healthy. Your classes should be carefully planned, paced, and medically approved. These people need exercise, but they can't keep up with a regular aerobics class. You also will find that you have a very devoted group of people who support and motivate each other. The members of this group, more than any other group, seem to become "regulars." An exercise group can become a social gathering. Not only does exercising help them physically, but emotionally as well.

As Isadore Rossman, M.D., Ph.D., states in the foreword to Magda Rosenberg's book, *Sixty Plus and Fit Again,* "Until recent years, the many benefits of exercise were not fully appreciated, even in medical circles. We now know that exercise programs can be of inestimable value; they have reached the status of medical prescription for some disorders like chronic backache, certain forms of heart disease, and chronic fatigue states." Rossman also states that, "Atrophy or disuse [a shrinkage of muscles and the weakness that follow as a consequence of non-use] is a well-known in geriatric medicine. Such atrophy can affect the joints the muscles act upon, resulting in stiffness of the joints and severe limitations of motion. In many older, sedentary people, stiffness and decreased mobility of joints are too readily attributed to 'age' or 'arthritis' when, in fact, it is poor conditioning which is often reversed promptly by exercise."

In her book *Sixty Plus and Fit Again,* Magda Rosenberg advises the following for participants:

1. It is never wise to impair your blood circulation at any time, especially during exercise. Don't wear tight-fitting clothing that might impede circulation.
2. Exercise in a cool room wearing light, loose clothing.
3. Don't exercise after eating.
4. Start your exercise program slowly.
5. *Never,* at the peak of exercising, decide that you deserve a rest and sit down.

In order to prevent a cardiovascular accident or musculoskeletal injury, a dance-exercise program must be carefully tailored to the health requirements of the student. There are three guidelines that leaders of exercise programs should follow. Richard Lopez described them as follows in the May 1983 *Journal of Physical Education.*

Recreation and Dance

1. Prospective students should have completed a thorough medical examination that assesses their ability to engage in progressively increasing intensities of exercise.
2. The type, intensity, duration, frequency, and progression of exercise should be prescribed according to each participant's physical capacity.
3. The teacher *must* define and practice an emergency plan, have someone trained in CPR present at every exercise session, and teach participants how to monitor their heart rates and identify signs of overexertion (dizziness, angina, nausea, breathing difficulty, and unusual fatigue or pain). The instructor should also watch for any signs of staggering, facial expressions that may signify severe distress, loss of vigor, or severe pallor. Emergency procedures and phone numbers should be posted.

With this type of participant, it is advisable to give each one a form that explains the content of your classes. The clients should take the forms to their physicians. If the physician who signs the form comments on anything, you should be aware of all such information concerning the student's health.

Make sure you have recent heart rate records that are both available and visible for each of your students. Heartbeats should not exceed 110–120 beats per minute, as this approaches the maximum heart rate for most elderly people.

The older participant may have sensory (hearing or sight) loss and/or mild physical handicaps. It is important for them to be able to hear your cues and to see you demonstrate steps. Try to keep your music at a moderate level. Check to see if more repetitions of a step are necessary.

Many of your students may have hypertension (high blood pressure), painful arthritic joints, and difficulty translating verbal cues into physical movements. If your class is comprised exclusively of older participants, slow down. If ages are mixed, make sure the older students know they can walk instead of jog.

Dr. Ruth Lindsey, corrective therapist and physical educator at California State University at Long Beach, lists several important potential danger or problem areas to keep in mind for the older age group. Older students should *not* do the following:

- neck rolling
- neck hyperextension
- deep knee bends
- straight leg sit-ups or leg lifts
- medial rotation and adduction of the hip joints for people with hip joint replacement
- standing toe touches with legs bent or straight
- arm circling forward (arm circling should only be done backwards with the arms rotated laterally)

Sue Pizzo, director of a New Jersey aerobics program called "Seniors Sit and Fit," convinced her students that it was never too late to start exercising. The program began with a moderate, seated warm-up and moved on to a vigorous, seated warm-up. The students then stood behind chairs where they worked with partners for balance. Free movement around the floor lasted for fifteen minutes and included such dances as the polka, hora, or Irish jig, and routines using equipment like broom handles and beach balls. The session concluded with students sitting in the chairs doing relaxation and breathing exercises, sometimes holding hands for emotional support. To get the word out that these classes are available, she visited senior citizens homes and apartment complexes, religious groups, and nursing homes.

Toby McErlean, instructor for the YMCA in Pensacola, Florida, started "Chairobics" class, which is done entirely in chairs. It is based on Dorothy Chrismon's principles and book, *Body Recall.* Toby found that there wasn't a part of the body that couldn't be worked while sitting, and her class incorporates aerobics, stretching, flexibility, and strength principles.

Susan Adams, another YMCA instructor, began an innovative program called "Fresh Start." Her program is for elderly persons who want to make a fresh start in fitness, beginning exercisers, overweight persons, and those with health problems. Each participant works on an individual basis, training to her or his own desired fitness level. There is no age limit, but the program caters to those people who cannot keep up with a vigorous program.

Leslie Johnson of Rhythmic Aerobics offers the following tips for instructors:

1. Check to see if your music appeals to the older person. If not, consider adding a song from an earlier era. Roaring Twenties and Big Band music are sure winners.

2. Keep your warm-up gentle and extend the time spent stretching, if needed. Avoid exercises that might strain back

muscles and proceed slowly with floor work. Even older students who balk at floor exercises will eventually appreciate them as they begin to reap the benefits.

3. Achieving a sense of proficiency is important for the older adult who may initially lack confidence. Repeat dances often and bring their favorites back for review. Gauge more challenging steps against the familiar movements.

4. Probably the most important ingredients you contribute as a successful teacher of older adults is your personality, sense of fun, and warmth. You can't fail to attract students to a classroom whose atmosphere is filled with friendliness and encouragement.

A SUCCESSFUL OVERWEIGHT PROGRAM

The Body Works Aerobic Fitness Program for the obese was originally developed for a government-funded medical facility serving a native American population. The project's medical director needed a program for overweight patients, all of whom suffered from other medical conditions such as hypertension, diabetes, and coronary heart disease.

The program was designed by Marcy Brown and Russell Buss, M.D., a sports medicine specialist, with input from Carol Evans, a registered dietitian. They set the goals of developing a medically safe aerobics program that combined sensible nutrition, weight loss, plus health fitness information.

In this program, every participant undergoes a physical assessment that is repeated in six to eight weeks. It includes hydrostatic weighing (weighing in water) to determine body fat. It also includes pulse rates, blood pressure tests, body measurements, flexibility tests, a three-minute cardiac test, and muscular strength tests. The muscular strength tests are done after a person has been exercising for six to eight weeks.

Many of the people in this program have lowered their blood pressure. Diabetic participants reduced their insulin intake and many have lost inches and pounds. Everyone in the program has noted improvement in self-esteem and quality of life.

Tips for the Instructor of Overweight Clients

1. Make sure your participants fill out a health history form. Those on medication, such as high blood pressure medication, may have a heart rate that is lower than normal during exercise. It is very important for you to be aware of these people and note any change in their medication.

2. Due to the high incidence of high blood pressure and diabetes in overweight participants, ask these clients to arrive thirty minutes before to have their blood pressure, blood sugar, and heart rate tested.

3. The overweight client requires a lot of attention. This may be the first time many of your participants have exercised. They tire easily, their heart rates elevate quickly, and it takes them longer to get up from the floor. Be sure to give alternate movements for each exercise if needed. You could also provide chairs to assist them in getting up from the floor.

4. Overweight participants are self-conscious about their size. You can make them feel more comfortable if they are

allowed to wear loose clothing instead of a leotard. You, too, should dress in warm-ups or shorts and a T-shirt instead of a leotard.

5. Provide motivation for your participants in the form of rewards, special events, or a bulletin board that lists student accomplishments.

If your program is for older, overweight, or out-of-shape students, remember that your encouragement and emotional support is as important as the physical routine itself.

CHAPTER 11

OWNING YOUR OWN GROUP-EXERCISE BUSINESS

ATTRACTING CLIENTS

An owner of a small fitness facility may know a lot about exercise, but very little about how to market and promote business. Most owners of studios understand the need for advertising in a highly competitive market, but many will go broke despite a good location and the ability to offer a quality class. The costs of professional advertising and promotion can be beyond your means, but you will save hundred of dollars if you take the time to make phone calls, write letters, and duplicate a few news releases yourself. These personal-touch endeavors can pay off tremendously and may bring even greater success than if you had had your advertisement prepared professionally.

Some marketing tips to help you promote your fitness business at a minimal cost are as follows:

1. First you must *know your market* and potential customers. What makes your studio unique in comparison to others

within a five-mile radius? Why will clients want to attend your classes instead of another studio's classes? What is the average fitness level of your students, their age group, the proportion of women to men? Keep track of any changes in client type and number to understand why your market has shifted.

2. What type of client attends your classes? In order to *know what media to target,* you need to know what and who your market is watching, listening to, and reading.

3. If you have newsworthy items to share with the public, *broadcasting* is an excellent media. Broadcast schedules may have spaces in their day for informative fitness bulletins. This also establishes your creditability in the community.

4. One of the best ways to draw attention to your studio is with an ad in your local *Yellow Pages.* Next, a *news release* should be sent to your local newspaper. This should be repeated every two to six months if there are updates you need to make the public aware of. For instance, if you are planning to sponsor a special program for an organization such as the American Heart Association, you should send news releases to all the local newspapers and magazines. Sponsoring new and different events is also an excellent promotional idea.

5. The most important factor to keep in mind is that the business you are promoting is one that is needed by the public. If you're enthusiastic and believe in your studio, people will listen.

RELEASE INFORMATION

As the most basic sales vehicle, the news release features timely news items for your studio. Even though all you write may not make it on the air or in print, in order for your news release to be read, you need to follow some simple guidelines. The first page of the news release should be brief and include only the most pertinent information. (See the example of the standard news release that follows.) This can be followed by more detailed information. Type and double-space an original announcement on your own letterhead, making sure there are no errors. Be sure you have your name and telephone number in the upper right-hand corner so that readers can contact you if necessary. At the top of the page, you also should type the release date, keeping it as current as possible.

In the first paragraph, you should include the complete name of the featured person, program, or organization. Then provide specific information about who the person is, or what the event is plus where and when it will take place.

In the second paragraph, underscore the importance of your featured person or organization with a significant fact. Then quote the most prominent person associated with the project; direct the quotation to the most significant readers. The quotation should attract their interest and cause them to pay closer attention to what they are reading. If you are targeting the release to a specific media source (the most common), introduce the name of the publication into this paragraph, too.

The next paragraph should give additional significant information about the person, organization, or event being featured. You can add here another noteworthy fact. If this release is about a person, you could add a quote that he or she made here.

STANDARD NEWS RELEASE

Contact: Name, Title

_____

Organization or Company

_____

Address

_____

Business Phone _____

Home Phone _____

Release Date _____

Summary Headline

_____

_____

_____

(The summary headline should be typed in all caps and give
  leading facts about the story.)

Date: City of origin

_____

In the fourth paragraph, you can add information of interest to the public that you are attempting to attract, such as significant facts or a quotation by a known authority.

If you add further paragraphs, you may want to let your readers know what you want them to do as a result of reading your story. Include all information about how the reader can get involved. One of the main things to keep in mind is to just quote the facts as you know them.

The news release can be developed into a feature story to spark human interest on a broader scale. Therefore, ask your media sources if they would be interested in doing a feature story on your news item. You may generate enough interest for the editor to assign the story to one of the reporters. Send the news release to as many sources as possible.

KEEPING CLIENTS

Now that you have attracted your clients, how do you keep them coming back to your class? Here are some helpful hints:

1. Everyone loves personal attention to their specific needs. For instance, if you have older clients in your class that feel as though they are not keeping up with the younger ones, you might compliment them on their particular improvements. In addition you should remind any beginning or special (overweight, medically impaired, and so forth) students to pace themselves and "listen to their body." Pacing means to exercise a little slower than the rest of the class. A person will do the same exercises, but may not go through as many

repetitions. Your main point to anyone in your class is that they should breathe as they exercise. Listening to their body is always stressed in a class because everyone is an individual and not everyone can keep up the same pace. For instance, if someone has a bad back, there are certain exercises that they should avoid. Another example, would be an overweight person. You need to pay particular attention to overweight people, because they are often so anxious to lose weight that they tend to overexercise. Overexercising in an overweight individual, or in any individual who enters your class in an unhealthy state, could lead to a heart attack. This is why we also stress that you should have knowledge in cardiopulmonary resuscitation and first aid.

2. You may find that some of your clients love your class, but they cannot afford to attend as much as they would want to. In many parts of the country there is a system called *bartering.* To give an example, one person may have needlework or woodworking skills. Another person may own chickens. The first person would barter with the second for some eggs by trading a pillow they embroidered or candlestick they made. You would be surprised how many interesting barters you can make with clients. You may find that you enjoy some of your "deals" more than what you would receive in money.

3. One of the best ways to keep clients coming back is to make your class a unique one. This can be accomplished in many ways. One way is to have special deals available. For instance, if participants pay ahead for a month's worth of classes at three classes a week, you give them an extra free class each week. Another idea is to have prizes for the "one

that breathed the best" or the "one who paced the best" or the "one who lost the most weight." The last suggestion, of course, would apply only to a special class in which many of your clients are striving for a similar goal, e.g., weight watchers. A prize could be given to the person who wore the funniest T-shirt at your T-shirt contest class. Providing your students with a variety of music is always important. For special occasions, you could have a fifties rock 'n' roll theme. If participants dress with a fifties flair, you could give a special prize. Many stores in your vicinity would love to give you coupons for a free yogurt, for example, to promote their product. So it's really not too difficult to obtain prizes for your students. Other prizes might be snazzy shoelaces, headbands, or socks. You may want to give a free class to a client who brings a new person into your classroom. You could also have a "free night." This is a great idea to introduce yourself to the community. Once the public experiences how much fun they can have in your class, they'll be coming back for more.

OWNING A STUDIO

Job Description

Owning your own studio is very exciting, but also very demanding on your time. It is not unusual to spend up to fourteen hours a day at your business. Functions include offering classes to the public, teaching classes and other instructors, managing the business and employees, maintenance, and promotion and advertising of the studio.

Education

Before considering opening your own business, it is advisable to have the experience of several years as a dance-exercise instructor and choreographer. You should have an understanding of exercise physiology and be trained and certified as a group-exercise instructor by a qualified organization. It also is desirable to have knowledge of business management, as this could determine the success or failure of your studio.

What Does It Cost to Get Started?

Even for a small operation, you should have at least $20,000, or enough to cover your expenses for one full year. These costs will include rent, studio renovation, advertising and promotion, office supplies, mailing and copying costs, in addition to employees' salaries, accountants' fees, insurance, and lawyers. It may take at least a year or two before you start to make a profit. Keep in mind that many studios go out of business in six months due to the competition in the market at present, and you will need a period of time to become established, develop your program, and build up your clientele.

Income

Income depends upon the size of the studio and the number of members. An approximate income for a moderate-size single studio with approximately twenty students at each class would be $40,000.

SATELLITE CLASSES

Job Description

In operating satellite classes, you basically operate your own business, but you don't own or rent the building that you use. You and those you hire teach at various locations like community centers, YMCAs, JCCs, health clubs, dance studios, and corporate centers. You manage the business aspect of your job in another facility, be it office space you rent or space you maintain in your own home. Your other duties include instructor training and choreography. Coordinating instructors and facilities can take up a lot of time. You can expect to work up to fourteen hours a day, six days a week, handling hiring, training, accounting, bookkeeping, program planning, and more.

Education

You should have experience as a group-exercise instructor and choreographer. You should have a knowledge of anatomy and physiology with certification as a group-exercise instructor and in CPR. A course in business management is advisable. If one of your satellite programs is at a corporation or hospital for its employees, it is recommended that you have a bachelor's, master's, or doctoral degree in exercise physiology, kinesiology, or sports medicine, especially if you are going to be doing fitness testing.

Because you will be offering your classes in someone else's facility, you may find that the organization has particular goals in mind for which you may need to be prepared.

CORPORATE PROGRAM

Job Description

Top management support is essential before beginning a wellness program in a corporation, and it is critical that this support continue for at least five years. The value of these programs must be understood by the major decision makers in the company, so that the program's continuing life will be a priority in the overall management plan. Anything short of complete support will increase the possibility of lack of acceptance by employees or failure of the program for other reasons.

Interest in fitness programs among senior management may be created in a number of ways; one of the most effective is by showing them the results of cardiovascular risk evaluation questionnaires, self-administered by employees, which identify a significant number of individuals with a high risk of cardiovascular disease. Demonstrating the success of other fitness programs in other corporations may also be helpful.

The program goals must be realistic and specific. Such broad goals as "health care cost containment through individual health management" are difficult to measure or attribute to a fitness program. To be realistic, goals must have well-defined content and time periods. When specific goals and objectives that are consistent with corporate goals have been defined, the program can be designed. Personnel, facilities, and the program itself should be considered.

You must be able to communicate to employees the importance of physical fitness and to motivate individuals to participate. You should also be able to set an example by practicing a lifestyle of exercising regularly, being moderate in alcohol use, not smoking, and not being overweight. If this fitness profile is not maintained, the credibility of the program suffers.

Once top management support has been enlisted and a plan with appropriate personnel, facilities, and products has been designed, action must be taken to effectively implement the fitness program. Initially there should be an employee orientation to the program that presents the reasons for being fit and the potential benefits.

If the goals and objectives are clearly defined in terms of content and time duration, and if adequate, accurate, and timely data have been collected on the effects on the participants and the program costs, the next steps are to select the evaluator and the evaluation methods.

One approach to evaluation is for the sponsoring management, the fitness program director, and the participating employees to develop the evaluation methods at the time they define the goals and objectives of the program. Their involvement in this dynamic process will result in their understanding and making a commitment to the program components. As the goals and objectives are strengthened by periodic evaluation and the participants interact in a flexible format, the success of the process becomes evident.

The President's Council on Physical Fitness and Sports has suggested several criteria that an employee fitness program should attempt to meet:

- The program should be an adjunct of the company's health program.
- It should include a medically oriented screening test as a criterion for participation.
- A person skilled in prescribing exercise should direct it.

- Exercise should be tailored to the individual participant and should be progressively more strenuous, in order to produce maximum benefits.
- Activities should be noncompetitive; individuals should compete only against their own person, not against other participants in the program.
- A system of periodic evaluation should be included to measure progress and to aid in program design.

Regardless of what other elements might be included in the planning of the health fitness program, the trend in business and industry is definitely toward expanding participation to include all levels of employees, rather than just executives. Also it is becoming accepted that, when possible, the program should be conducted on company time to increase motivation. At the least, employees should have a wide selection of possible times for participating.

Finally, it is a good idea to publish a regular newsletter to promote interest in the program. The newsletter should publish schedules for use of facilities and upcoming classes as well as seminars and other group activities. It is also an excellent chance to increase health awareness, through special columns written by experts on various subjects such as weight management, hypertension control, and stress reduction.

Education

The corporation program director should have previous experience or specialized training in health fitness management and in data processing and statistical analysis. The fitness director must be experienced in the techniques of exercise testing and prescription and have knowledge of the physiological response to exercise and various stress testing protocols. Training in emergency procedures, including cardiopulmonary resuscitation and basic life support, is essential. Also specific experience or training in education or counseling is invaluable. These skills and experiences might be found among physicians, nurses, or those with special training in exercise physiology, physical education, or health fitness management.

What Does It Cost to Get Started?

If you are starting a consulting program for corporations, as fitness instructor your start-up costs can run from $15,000 to $500,000 depending on staffing, insurance, and equipment needed. You should seek legal advice immediately, as well as contact insurance companies. It also can take several months of promoting your program to companies before you get started, so you should have enough financial backing to pay all your expenses.

Company physical fitness facilities vary in scope and cost. Facilities for an on-site program should provide, as a minimum, showers, locker rooms, and a meeting room for educational programs. The cost of a minimal on-site program is about $250 per participant per year. Companies may provide off-site fitness programs at the local YMCA or local health clubs with the cost paid in full or shared with the employee. Some companies provide a health insurance premium deduction for employees who regularly attend the exercise program.

A comprehensive on-site program would provide rooms for stretching and aerobic dance classes as well as for stationary bicycles, treadmills, stair-climbing machines, weight training equipment, bench presses, and leg equipment and abdominal machines, at the very least. Cost estimates for comprehensive programs range from $450 to $1,000 per participant per year. Besides the equipment necessary for testing and exercise, data processing is essential for management and analysis. Computer terminals placed at the exercise facility enable employees to receive immediate feedback on their progress. Data processing is critical for developing a database and for accurate individual and group assessment.

Income

Income is consistent with what you would make if you owned your own studio or operated a satellite class, taking into consideration the number of participants, how many classes you teach, and what you charge per class. An income can range between $15,000 and $50,000 per year.

Additional Information

Association for Worksite Health Promotion
   60 Revere Drive, Suite 500
   Northbrook, IL 60062

   (Formerly the Association for Fitness in Business)

INCOME TAXES

Taxes vary according to personal financial habits, state laws, and individual tax brackets. The guidelines below may help you to minimize taxes.

Label a large manilla envelope "Taxes." There are also specially designed envelopes for this purpose, which can be found in any stationery shop. For each check or charge, be sure to include the amount, time, place and business purpose of your expenditure. Make sure you get receipts for all your business-related purchases. Put all your receipts into this one place and at the end of the year, you will have all your documentation together. Thus, it is important to be organized.

Keep an account book for jotting down all your various transactions that are business related. A few minutes each day could save hours of frustration at the end of the year.

Deductions can be extensive and confusing. Visit a tax expert who will provide you with any necessary specific information. Business deductions you can use are education, travel, meals, and lodging (for example, attending a dance-exercise seminar). Other general business expenses you can deduct are supplies such as exercise mats, running shoes, tape recorders, and compact discs.

After you have calculated your business deductions, you now have your adjusted gross income. It is a financial plateau between certain deductions you are allowed to take. This figure is necessary to compute the second set of deductions you are allowed by law.

Now that you know your adjusted gross income, you can list your next group of deductions. These deductions are called "itemized deductions," and they are subtracted from your adjusted gross income to arrive at your "taxable income." These items may include certain medical expenses, charitable contributions, and interest expenses. The tax rate depends on the individual and your personal situation.

The above material should help you become aware of how to prepare for reporting your tax situation. It is recommended, though, that professional consultation with a tax accountant or tax consultant be sought as the tax law is extensive and complex, and it is important to be accurate and complete in handling your records.

INSURANCE

Insurance is your business's protection. The moment you establish a business, you have also established the need for insurance. Fitness instructors need to protect themselves from potential liability claims, and you are particularly vulnerable to such claims if you own your own business.

Comprehensive general liability insurance protects individuals, professionals, and businesses from various liability hazards resulting from owned, leased, or otherwise occupied premises. With this insurance, the instructor of the class would have coverage for any injuries or damages if negligence were proven on her or his part.

Incidental professional liability insurance protects you from malpractice claims by any of your instructors, employees, or volunteers for bodily injury arising out of the performance of, or failure to perform, professional services. If an injury does occur, this coverage will protect you from an expensive lawsuit.

Additional named insurance coverage is especially important if you are teaching in a municipality, large commercial center, after-school club, or a school district. It enables the landlords to be protected for their contingent liability for your acts.

Personal injury coverage protects you against suits involving slander, libel, and defamation of character, as well as false arrest and invasion of privacy. The coverage applies both to you and your employees.

Below is a partial list of other coverages that may be equally important to you. The insurance industry is constantly creating new types of coverage. Find an experienced broker or agent to help you meet your needs.

Worker's Compensation
Contractual Liability
Fire Legal Liability
Property Insurance
Automobile Insurance
Bonds
Major Medical and Hospitalization
Life Insurance
Disability
Dental
Accident

Because the insurance needs of every business are specific, you will need to consult with a professional insurance service to ensure the most adequate and economical coverage for you.

CHAPTER 12

TECHNOLOGY—
THE TOUGH TRAINER

What are technological trainers and what do they have to do with health fitness? More than you could ever have imaged. With the help of a computer, you can now balance your diet, discover what is wrong with your exercise program, and simply inspire yourself to stay fit.

With the aid of computerized machines, fitness trainers and others are better equipped to evaluate muscular strength, flexibility, cardiovascular endurance, and percentage of body fat. Usually the exercise regimen is developed by a club trainer in consultation with the client, but sometimes the trainer gets assistance from the computer. Many clubs today are using computer programs to store client information, such as interests, times available, and fitness scores. Using these data, the computer designs an exercise prescription that takes into account such information as the client's cardiovascular status, weight, medical history, dietary intake, and goals to provide the client with a safe program.

There are machines today that weigh your food and tell you the amount of sodium, carbohydrates, protein, cholesterol, fat, and calorie content for almost any food portion. With the aid of this computerized device, you can keep track of your total food consumption for a day. There are also computer programs that tell you how much exercise it takes to burn off the calories you've consumed. Basically, with the great variety of fitness programs available, it sometimes takes a computer software package to do the analysis and tell you the best method to use.

Obviously, with the advent of these electronic trainers, there is a need in the health fitness industry for individuals who understand and enjoy designing, programming, and operating these technological tools. Learning how to operate a computer or any other complex device requires either on-the-job training or study in a trade school or a college-level fitness program. Serving as a health fitness consultant for software developers is also an excellent opportunity for people with advanced degrees in exercise physiology, nutrition, kinesiology, and related disciplines.

If you would rather be in a job behind the scenes, this rapidly growing industry might utilize your skills in the development of programs or devices. But even if you prefer interacting with others and working directly with the public, it's still best to get some exposure to computers due to the impact technology has made on this ever-growing industry.

CHAPTER 13

KEEPING UP WITH THE CHANGES

Conferences on a variety of health fitness topics are held throughout the year in all parts of the country. Announcements of many meetings and seminars can be found in issues of *IDEA Today* and *Sports Medicine Bulletin,* to name but two. You should certainly contact the Sport Information Resource Centre (SIRC) on the Internet at http://www.sirc.ca/index.html for listings of conferences around the globe. Or, you can receive additional information by writing to SIRC directly (see Appendix A). Many of these conferences are hosted by colleges and universities, while others take place at hotels or spas and are coordinated by health fitness organizations.

Conferences are an excellent opportunity to learn about current trends in the health fitness field. They provide valuable networking possibilities since you undoubtedly will meet hundreds of other professionals. Each discipline within the health fitness constellation has its own conferences. There are occupational therapy conferences, physical therapy conferences, weight training conferences, sports medicine conferences, and many others. You should read the prospectus of any conferences you wish to attend to see if the focus and format will be of interest to you.

Trade shows are also a good resource. At trade shows you will see the latest equipment and technology, clothing and accessories, books and videos, and any other items that may be helpful to you.

Because the industry is expanding so rapidly, it is essential that you continue to update your knowledge. It is equally important for you to maintain contacts in the profession. Conferences, seminars, workshops, professional publications, and graduate courses contribute to sources of additional education, training, and refresher courses.

In 1973 the Presidential Sports Award and Fitness Leadership Program was initiated. It is a fitness motivation program directed to the fitness and aerobic exercise industry. The Presidential Sports Award and Fitness Leadership Program is a program of the President's Council on Physical Fitness and Sports that seeks to motivate active and regular participation in sports and sports fitness activities. The program offers successful candidates who earn the Presidential Sports Award a wonderful opportunity to become fitness leaders and bring to their school, community, fitness facility, or club a prestigious motivational fitness ideology. In addition anyone who regularly participates in sports receives a certificate of achievement signed by the President of the United States, a lapel pin, and other award materials The council has established qualifying standards for forty-three activities. To qualify, participants must be fifteen years of age or older and have completed the requirements set for each activity within a period of four months. Although the award recognizes individual performance, the program can be used as a group motivational tool to encourage attendance and participation in employee fitness programs and other adult or youth fitness programs. To receive a personal fitness log and more information, send a stamped, self-addressed envelope to:

President's Council on Physical Fitness and Sports
  710 Pennsylvania Avenue, NW, Suite 205
  Washington, DC 20004

Continuing education, either in a formal academic setting or through the seminars and courses offered by professional associations, has become an important aspect of career advancement. Opportunities to attend workshops, seminars, and trade shows are skyrocketing. Peers are likely to be taking courses, and because the industry is changing so fast, continuing education is needed if you want to stay current and employable.

Competition, specialization, and diversification have caught up with the fitness industry. Formal training, academic degrees, and access to the latest information on market trends and management techniques have become the essential tools that give employees a professional edge.

CHAPTER 14

CHOREOGRAPHY
AND MUSIC SERVICES

CHOREOGRAPHY

Choreography is the art of designing dance steps to music. Choreographing fitness activities can be fun, but it does require hours of preparation. The dilemma in creating a routine for an exercise program is to keep the abilities of your participants in mind. Some of them may be athletes, while others may be elderly, pregnant, or simply have "two left feet." If routines are not simplified and changed on a frequent basis, you may lose a class to frustration or boredom. A routine can easily be altered by such devices as changing arm movements, or by lifting the spirits with new music, especially if the participants can sing along. Playing "sing along" music is advantageous as you can assess how participants are doing, by seeing if they are able to talk to the persons near them, or if you notice them singing to the tune on the cassette player. In addition to making routines more enjoyable, exercising with music makes it easier to remember the steps to the routine and keeps the class together.

Listed here are several points to remember when you are the choreographer for a health fitness class:

1. Your sense of rhythm and timing is vital. You must always know where the beat of the music is and never lose it.

2. Choose a variety of music because everyone has a favorite type of music. Music is probably the number one motivator of most students. If your exercise style tends more to jazz type movements, your music should center on the jazz/ R&B/soul. If you tend more toward an athletic style, your music should probably lean toward harder rock and pop songs. Pop/county, soft rock, and old time rock 'n roll are good if you are teaching senior citizens, children, or a class with many types of individuals. In all cases, change your music frequently to avoid boredom.

3. In evaluating each song you choose, divide it into parts. Each part will have different sets of eight counts. Try to keep the tune divided into no more than five parts and repeat the same movements when the music repeats itself. This simplifies the routine.

4. The energy and spirit of your music should match the energy and spirit of the exercises and steps you do and also should correspond with your style of teaching.

5. Once you have an outline of what you want to do, check the routine for smoothness of transitions. Also check for the correctness of body alignment. Make sure you are using both sides of the body to exercise the muscles more effectively.

6. Add arm movements to help the routine flow, stressing to the student the placement of the arm in order to work the

arm muscles more effectively. During warm-up and cool down, the arm movements should be of lower intensity while during peak time, they should be of higher intensity.

If you wish to improve your routine or if you have never choreographed an exercise class, attend classes taught by highly recommended instructors. Observe not only the teacher, but the people in the class. Is the spirit high and the music motivating? Is everyone following the routine easily, in unison, and with good form? Are the transitions clean and do you like the teacher's style? Most importantly, was the whole body worked evenly from head to toe? When designing your program, make sure to reevaluate it periodically. Listen to your clients, and think about what they say. If they complain and drop out, there may be something you can do to improve the class. If they grow more fit, and bring new clients to class, be sure you know what has been successful. The key to a good class is meeting the needs of your clients.

MUSIC SERVICES

There are choreography and music services available if you think what they offer is what you need for your class. Services offered include original music, choreography, videotapes, and voice programs. Keep in mind that an instructor has the right to ascertain precisely what he or she is buying for a music service. A legitimate organization should have absolutely no difficulty explaining from whom and in what manner its rights were obtained. Local music services are listed in the *Yellow Pages* under "aerobics" or "exercise and physical fitness programs."

LEGAL LIMITATIONS

Many instructors prefer to make their own tapes for their classes since they find that most records and tapes on the market are not appropriate to their routines or their clientele. Exercise instructors need to be aware, though, of the legal limits of taping popular music for dance exercise classes.

Under the 1976 Copyright Act, the creator or owner of certain types of original musical compositions is afforded certain exclusive rights to exploit such works and certain concomitant protection against unauthorized persons doing so. There is no prohibition against or license required in connection with the performance of a sound recording itself. Therefore, if you just wanted to play the album or commercially issued tape in an exercise class, without copying it onto another tape, or if you were willing to record and use a "sound alike" version, you would have to obtain a license from the publisher of the song, but would not have to obtain permission form the record company. The license needed to record a musical composition, called a "mechanical" license, costs only a few cents per song per tape, and the performing license needed to play or otherwise perform the composition in class can generally be obtained inexpensively, frequently on an overall basis, from one of the two performing rights societies, ASCAP and BMI, which represent music publishers in negotiating and collecting performance fees. The music services which manufacture and supply "sound alike" recordings presumably have obtained the right to do so by securing the necessary mechanical and performing licenses from the applicable publishers. Thus, an individual facility or club could probably obtain the necessary performing licenses to permit the playing of musical compositions by means of unduplicated commercial recordings. It is advisable, for your own protection, to seek legal advice before choreographing your class. IDEA, The International Association of Fitness Professionals, listed in Chapter 15, also can provide you with updated information on the legalities associated with music use.

CHAPTER 15

SOME PROFESSIONAL ORGANIZATION AND TRAINING CENTER PROFILES

Professional organizations and training centers have been developed in increasing numbers to provide resources and information. As will be seen in Appendix A, "North American Health Fitness Organizations," the list is large and ever-growing. This chapter profiles selected professional organizations in order to give you a better understanding of the health fitness industry. The inclusion or exclusion of any particular organization does not indicate it is recommended over any other; rather, economy of space does not allow for a detailed look at every organization. It's up to you to carry out the research you need to make an informed career choice, but this chapter should give you an idea at what to look for. For a comprehensive listing of professional organizations, see Appendix A.

The Cooper Aerobics Center
  1220 Preston Road
  Dallas, TX 75230
  http://www.cooperinst.org/

The Cooper Aerobics Center acts as the umbrella organization to its various divisions. The Cooper Institute for Aerobics Research is the nonprofit arm of the Cooper Aerobics Center founded by Kenneth H. Cooper, M.D., M.P.H., to establish scientific methods for prescribing safe and effective exercise for health enhancement. The Institute's Division of Continuing Education offers education and consultation programs that directly translate what is learned through Center projects into practice in the field. One major effort is the development of a program for attaining a certificate of proficiency in the "Management of Exercise and Fitness Programs." The purpose of this workshop and certificate program is to provide trainers with an opportunity to study, in depth, the management of exercise and fitness programs. Another major thrust that the Institute's Continuing Education Division is currently engaged in is consulting in the area of fitness program development. Besides conducting needs assessment and master plans and developing programs for individual organizations, The Cooper Aerobics Center has developed a unique employee educational package called *Fitness: The Facts.* It is a communicative program consisting of six books on the basics of maintaining a medically safe and sound fitness program. A computer software program that serves as an exercise log feedback system also has been developed.

Another portion of the Cooper Aerobics Center is the Aerobics Activity Center, the Center's health club. The Cooper Clinic is the preventive medicine center of the Cooper Aerobics Center, where you can gain certification as an exercise instructor after you meet their requirements. The staff of the Aerobics Center has written may articles that you can find in various journals and magazines. They hold seminars as well as weekly workshops on health fitness. They also provide a newsletter on medical updates for their members and clients.

American College of Sports Medicine (ACSM)
P.O. Box 1440
Indianapolis, IN 46206

(Home page is under construction at time of writing.)

The ACSM is a nonprofit, multidisciplinary, professional, and scientific society dedicated to the generation and dissemination of knowledge concerning the motivations, responses, adaptations, and overall health aspects of persons engaged in sports and exercise. Membership comprises more than forty medical and scientific specialties including exercise physiology, cardiac and respiratory rehabilitation, physical education, athletic training, physical therapy, and physical fitness. Membership offers educational opportunities, forums for presenting scientific research through meetings and publications, and professional recognition through certification in special skills areas, awards, and advancement to Fellowship status. The College is affiliated with the American Alliance for Health, Physical Education, Recreation and Dance; the United States Olympic Committee; the President's Council on Physical Fitness and Sports; and the American Medical Association Committee on the Medical Aspects of Sports.

American Dance Therapy Association (ADTA)
2000 Century Plaza, Suite 108
Columbia, MD 21044
http://www.social.com/health/nhic/data/hr1800/hr1806.html

ADTA stimulates communication among dance/movement therapists and members of allied professionals through publication of the *ADTA Newsletter,* the *American Journal of Dance*

Therapy, monographs, bibliographies, and conference proceedings. ADTA holds an annual conference and supports formation of regional groups, conferences, seminars, workshops, and meetings throughout the year. The association has always distinguished between dance/movement therapists prepared to work in professional settings within a team or under supervision, and those prepared for the responsibilities of working independently in solo practice.

Aerobics and Fitness Association of America (AFAA)
    15250 Ventura Boulevard, Suite 301
    Sherman Oaks, CA 01493
    http://www.cybercise.com/

A professional organization for physical fitness trainers, aerobic exercise instructors, and enthusiasts that provides certification, education, and training programs plus an international membership association. Certification culminates in the receipt of the AFP, the AFAA Fitness Practitioner Certification, which is awarded after a rigorous study and examination program. AFAA also is committed to research, product evaluation, and the study of aerobic exercise and fitness. Members receive a health insurance plan for personal liability insurance; *American Fitness Journal*; professional discounts; AFAA book and videos; discounts on air fares, hotels, and car rentals; membership card, decal, and certificate; plus information on workshops, seminars, and continuing education. Each year they hold APEX, a four-day fitness conference for aerobic professionals, fitness leaders, and fitness enthusiasts. They also have developed videotapes including, "AFAA's Basic Exercise Standards and Guidelines" and "Strength Training and the Use of Light Weights." By August 1996, more than 70,000 fitness professionals in the United States and in seventy-three other countries earned AFAA primary certification.

IDEA, The International Association of Fitness Professionals
   6190 Cornerstone Court East, Suite 204
   San Diego, CA 92121-3773
   http://www.ideafit.com

IDEA, The International Association of Fitness Professionals, formerly the International Dance-Exercise Association, is a trade association for professional trainers and fitness program directors. IDEA publishes numerous information resources, among them *IDEA Today,* an important magazine for fitness professionals; industry reports; *IDEA Personal Trainer* magazine; and *IDEA Fitness Manager* newsletter. Benefits of membership include, in addition to the informative publications, the IDEA annual directory and information concerning pertinent products and services, professional liability insurance at reduced group rates, and product discounts. IDEA also is involved in promoting research and wellness through its consumer publications.

Jazzercise
   2808 Roosevelt Street
   Carlsbad, CA 92008
   http://www.jazzercise.com

Jazzercise was started in 1969 as a total body conditioning program combining the flow and rhythm of dance with the basic principles of exercise physiology. Jazzercise has set an industry standard with a top quality instructors' training program. Instructors must pass an intensive training workshop, which provides instruction in dance techniques and terminology, human anatomy, and physiology. They must be CPR certified annually and are continually monitored as teachers. Through regional workshops and conventions, videocassettes, and company newsletters, instructors take part in the continuing exercise physiology and safety education started by Jazzercise. Classes are offered to more than

400,000 students in all fifty states, and fifteen other countries including Canada, Australia, and Italy. Jazzercise currently services an estimated 3,000 individually owned franchises that are overseen by the corporate offices. Instructors receive the benefits of business ownership while enjoying support from the corporation through ongoing training materials and national advertising. The facility encompasses a broadcast-quality videotape operation, warehousing for Jazzercise records and tapes, and a Jazzertogs line of leotards, warm-up suits, T-shirts, and shoes.

National Athletic Trainer's Association (NATA)
2952 Stemmons Freeway
Dallas, TX 75247
http://www.nata.org/

NATA is a nonprofit organization "dedicated to improving the health and wellness of athletes around the world." NATA's membership comprises more than 21,000 personal trainers, approximately 92 percent of certified professionals, of whom 40 percent are women.

NATA-certified trainers have earned at least a bachelor's degree in training, health fitness, physical education, or exercise physiology. They continue to study and work in the field and receive certification only after passing a rigorous examination.

National Federation of Professional Trainers (NFPT)
P.O. Box 4579
Lafayette, IN 47903-4570
http://www.nfpt.com/nfpt/

Since 1988 the NFPT has sought to provide an "affordable, convenient, comprehensive, and applicable" educational program to exercise professionals, "offer organizational certification credentials for consumer recognition of competency," and provide other services to the health fitness field. The NFPT's educational program comprises a wide variety of reference materials, study guides, and videos to help you further develop your skills and abilities as a personal trainer. Three distinct levels of certification are offered by the NFPT, with each section consisting of 100 multiple choice and true/false questions. Members and/or NFPT Certified Personal Fitness Trainers receive the bimonthly magazine, *NFPT Personal Trainer Magazine,* and other materials of interest to fitness professionals. Professional liability is also offered through the organization.

National Strength and Conditioning Association (NSCA)
P.O. Box 38909
Colorado Springs, CO 80937-8909
http://colosoft.com/nsca

The NSCA was established in 1978 as a nonprofit educational organization. Its 12,000 members from around the world are dedicated fitness professionals interested in the scientific and practical/applied aspects of physical training. Members receive a bimonthly journal, a quarterly publication, and a bimonthly bulletin. Career information, conferences, and educational resources also are made available to members.

In 1985 the NSCA initiated its Strength and Condition Specialist (CSCS) award certification program as a way to identify individuals who have demonstrated the knowledge and skills necessary to design and implement safe and effective strength and conditioning programs. In 1993 the NCSA-Certified Personal Trainer Examination was created for professionals who train clients on a one-on-one setting in client homes, health and fitness clubs, and YMCAs.

NORTH AMERICAN HEALTH FITNESS ORGANIZATIONS

The organizations included here are among the many professional societies in any one of the three main branches of the health fitness field. For updated information refer to *National Trade and Professional Associations of the United States,* published by Columbia Books, Inc., as well as various trade magazines. Website locations are given when available. Like mailing addresses, these also change, so it may be necessary to run an Internet search to find the new address. In two instances, only electronic medium addresses are available. Persons with Internet access also should visit the various sites of the Sport Information Resource Centre, especially http://www.sirc.ca/usmed.html and http://www.sirc.ca/infocen.html.

Academy of Sport Psychology International
   6161 Bush Boulevard, #126
   Columbus, OH 43229

(Conducts and shares research exploring high-level performance under stress in order to condition psychological behavior for optimum athletic performance.)

Aerobics and Fitness Association of America (AFAA)
  15250 Ventura Boulevard, Suite 301
  Sherman Oaks, CA 01493
  http://www.cybercise.com/

Amateur Athletic Union
  AAU House
  3400 West Eighty-sixth Street
  Box 68207
  Indianapolis, IN 46268

American Academy of Orthotists and Prosthetists
  1650 King Street, Suite 500
  Alexandria, VA 22314
  http://www.oandp.com

American Academy of Osteopathy
  3500 DePaw Boulevard, Suite 1080
  Indianapolis, IN 46286

American Academy of Sports Physicians
  17113 Gledhill Street
  Northridge, CA 91325
  http://www.social.com/health/nhic/data/hr2100/hr2185.html

American Alliance for Health, Physical Education, Recreation,
    and Dance (AAHPERD)
  1900 Association Way
  Reston, VA 22091
  http://www.aahperd.org/

(Extensive archives and research data available to members.
Also publishes several journals.)

American Association for Active Lifestyles and Fitness
1900 Association Way
Reston, VA 22091
(Affiliate of AAHPERD.)

American Association of Cardiovascular and Pulmonary
    Rehabilitation
7611 Elmwood Avenue, Suite 201
Middletown, WI 53562

American Association of Colleges of Osteopathic Medicine
6110 Executive Boulevard, Suite 405
Rockville, MD 20852

American Association for Leisure and Recreation
1900 Association Way
Reston, VA 22091

(Affiliate of AAHPERD. Members are teachers of leisure studies, park administrators, park rangers and tour guides, counselors, and so forth.)

American Chiropractic Association
1701 Claredon Boulevard
Arlington, VA 22209
http://www.cais.net/aca/

American College of Nurse-Midwives
818 Connecticut Avenue, NW, Suite 900
Washington, DC 20006-2702

American College of Sports Medicine
P.O. Box 1440
Indianapolis, IN 46206-1440

American Council on Exercise
  5820 Oberlin Drive, Suite 102
  San Diego, CA 92121-3787

American Dance Therapy Association
  2000 Century Plaza, Suite 108
  10632 Little Patuxent Parkway
  Columbia, MD 21044-3263
  http://www.social.com/health/nhic/data/hr1800/hr1806.html

(Provides research opportunities to members and certification for dance therapy professionals.)

American Fitness Association
  P.O. Box 461
  Durango, CO 81302

(Grew out of the American Aerobics Association, which is itself now a division of the AFA. AFA is an umbrella organization for fitness research, with some 41,000 members. Annual meetings are held only in Durango, Colorado.)

American Heart Association
  National Center
  7272 Greenville Avenue
  Dallas, TX 75231-4596
  http://www.amhrt.org/

(Provides a wealth of qualitative and quantitative data for health fitness researchers and writers.)

American Kinesiotherapy Association
  P.O. Box 5188
  Vancouver, WA 98668

American Medical Athletic Association
  P.O. Box 4704
  North Hollywood, CA 91617

American Occupational Therapy Association
  P.O. Box 31220
  Bethesda, MD 20824-1220

American Orthopaedic Society for Sports Medicine
  6300 North River Road, Suite 200
  Rosemont, IL 60018

American Orthopedic Society for Sports Medicine
  1805 Park Street
  Box 824
  Middleton, WI 53562

American Osteopathic Academy of Sports Medicine
  7611 Elmwood Avenue, Suite 201
  Middleton, WI 53562

American Osteopathic Healthcare Association
  5301 Wisconsin Avenue, NW
  Washington, DC 30015

American Physical Therapy Association
  111 North Fairfax Street
  Alexandria, VA 22314
  http://www.apta.org

American Running and Fitness Association
  4405 E. West Highway
  Bethedsa, MD 20814

American Society of Biomechanics
    c/o Department of Biomechanical Engineering
    Cleveland Clinic Foundation
    9500 Euclid Avenue
    Cleveland, OH 44195

American Society of Hand Therapists
    401 North Michigan Avenue
    Chicago, IL 60611-4267

(Members are occupational or physical therapists working with patients with hand problems such as arthritis, repetitive strain disorders, injuries, and birth defects.)

American Sports Medicine Association
    660 West Duarte Road
    Arcadia, CA 91006

American Swimming Coaches Association
    1 Hall of Fame Drive
    Ft. Lauderdale, FL 33316

American Yoga Association
    513 South Orange Avenue
    Sarasota, FL 34236

Aquatic Exercise Association
    1032 South Spring Street
    P.O. Box 497
    Port Washington, WI 53074

Association for Worksite Health Promotion
    60 Revere Drive, Suite 500
    Northbrook, IL 60062
    http://www.awhp.com

(Formerly the Association for Fitness in Business. Membership comprises exercise facility managers, human resource directors, health educators, corporate wellness directors, personal trainers, and so forth. The organization currently has some 2,800 members, 1,000 of which attend annual meetings.)

Athletic Training Research and Education Society (ATRES)
  http://poe.acc.virginia.edu/~rjs5s/atres.html

Black Women in Sport Foundation
  P.O. Box 2610
  Philadelphia, PA 19130

Canadian Association for Health, Physical Education, Recreation, and Dance
  1600 James Naismith Drive
  Gloucester, Ontario
  K1B 5N4 Canada
  http://activeliving.ca/activeliving/cahperd/

Canadian Association of Occupational Therapists
  110 Eglinton Avenue West
  Toronto, Ontario
  M4R 1A3 Canada

Certified Pool Operators Association
  481 Beech Street
  Boston, MA 02131

Cooper Institute for Aerobic Research
  12330 Preston Road
  Dallas, TX 75230
  http://www.cooperinst.org/

Council for National Cooperation in Aquatics
910 West New York Street
Indianapolis, IN 46223

IDEA, The International Association of Fitness Professionals
6190 Cornerstone Court East, Suite 204
San Diego, CA 92121-3773
http://www.ideafit.com

International Kids' Fitness Association
27 West Twentieth Street, Suite 1207
New York, NY 10011

Jazzercise, Inc.
2808 Roosevelt Street
Carlsbad, CA 92008
http://www.jazzercise.com

National Academy of Sports Medicine
2434 North Greenview Avenue
Chicago, IL 60614

National Association for Girls and Women in Sports
1900 Association Drive
Reston, VA 22091

National Association for Human Development
http://social.com/health/nhic/data/index.html

National Association of Rehabilitation Instructors
633 South Washington Street
Alexandria, VA 22314

National Association for Sport and Physical Education
1900 Associate Drive
Reston, VA 22091

National Athletic Trainer's Association
  2952 Stemmons Freeway
  Dallas, TX 75247
  http://www.nata.org/

National Center for Health Fitness
  http://www.healthy.american.edu/nchf.html

National Federation of Professional Trainers
  P.O. Box 4579
  Lafayette, IN 47903-4570
  http://www.nfpt.com/nfpt/

National Handicapped Sports Association
  4405 E. West Highway, Suite 603
  Bethesda, MD 20814

National Institute for Fitness and Sport
  250 North University Boulevard
  Indianapolis, IN 46202-5192

National Strength and Conditioning Association
  P.O. Box 38909
  Colorado Springs, CO 80937
  http://colosoft.com.nsca

National Swim and Recreation Association
  429 Ridge Pike
  Lafayette Hill, PA 19444

National Therapeutic Recreation Society
  c/o National Recreation and Park Association
  2775 South Quincy Street
  Arlington, VA 22206
  http://www.nrpa.org

National Youth Sports Foundation for the Prevention of Athletic
    Injuries
    10 Meredith Circle
    Needham, MA 02192

President's Council on Physical Fitness and Sports
    701 Pennsylvania Avenue, NW, Suite 205
    Washington, DC 20004

Recreation Safety Institute
    P.O. Box 392
    Ronkonkoma, NY 11779

Road Runners Club of America—Sports Medicine Committee
    1150 South Washington Street, Suite 250
    Alexandria, VA 22314-4493

Sport Information Research Centre (SIRC)
    1600 James Naismith Drive
    Gloucester, Ontario
    K1B 5N4 Canada
    http://www.sirc.ca/

Sports Equipment Research Foundation
    11724 Plaza Circle
    P.O. Box 20626
    Kansas City, MO 64195

United States Water Fitness Association
    P.O. Box 3279
    Boynton Beach, FL 33424-2379
    http://www.emi.net/uswfa/

Women's Sports Foundation
    342 Madison Avenue, Suite 728
    New York, NY 10173

FURTHER READING

JOURNALS AND MAGAZINES

Newsstands abound with dozens of magazines pertaining to working out, jogging, swimming, aerobic exercise, and every conceivable sport. As a result of the plethora of materials, the recommendations provided here are mostly professional and scientific publications for the serious health fitness student. Frequency of publication is given wherever possible. Undoubtedly some fine publications inadvertently will have been omitted from this list, so check your local library for additional publications of high caliber.

Physiology, Physical Education, Sports

Advances: Journal of Mind-Body Health
Fetzer Institute
9292 West Kalamazoo Avenue
Kalamazoo, MI 49009-9398
(quarterly)

Advances in Physiology Education
   The American Physiology Society
   9650 Rockville Pike
   Bethedsa, MD 20814
   (2 times per year)

American Fitness
   15250 Ventura Boulevard, Suite 200
   Sherman Oaks, CA 91403
   (bimonthly)

American Health
   19 West Twenty-second Street
   New York, NY 10010
   (10 times per year)

Fitness Diet and Exercise Guide
   The Family Circle, Inc.
   110 Fifth Avenue
   New York, NY 10011
   (5 times per year)

Journal of Aging and Physical Activity
   Human Kinetics Publishers, Inc.
   607 North Market Street
   P.O. Box 5076
   Champaign, IL 61825-5076

Journal of Strength and Conditioning Research
   National Strength and Conditioning Association
   P.O. Box 38909
   Colorado Springs, CO 80937

Medicine and Science in Sports
   351 West Camden Street
   Baltimore, MD 21201-2434
   (monthly)

Research Quarterly for Exercise and Sport
    1900 Association Way
    Reston, VA 22091

Strategies
    (Journal of Physical Education and Recreation)
    1900 Association Way
    Reston, VA 22091
    (8 times per year)

Strength and Conditioning
    National Strength and Conditioning Association
    P.O. Box 38909
    Colorado Springs, CO 80937
    (bimonthly)

Kinesiotherapy and Physical and Occupational Therapy

American Journal of Occupational Therapy
    616 Tanner Mauk Road
    Guilford, CT 06437
    (monthly)

Canadian Journal of Applied Physical Therapy
    Human Kinetics Publishers, Inc.
    607 North Market Street
    P.O. Box 5076
    Champaign, IL 61825-5076
    (quarterly)

Canadian Journal of Occupational Therapy
    110 Eglinton Avenue West
    Toronto, Ontario
    M4R 1A3 Canada
    (monthly)

IDEA Today
   IDEA, The International Association of Fitness Professionals
   6190 Cornerstone Court East, Suite 204
   San Diego, CA 92121-3773

Journal of Electromyography and Kinesiology
   Liptencoct-Raven
   1185 Avenue of the Americas
   Mail Stop 3B
   New York, NY 10036
   (quarterly)

Magazine of Physical Therapy
   American Physical Therapy Association
   1111 North Fairfax Street
   Alexandria, VA 22314
   (monthly)

Occupational Therapy in Health Care
   The Haworth Press, Inc.
   10 Alice Street
   Binghamton, NY 13904-1580
   (quarterly)

Occupational Therapy in Mental Health
   The Haworth Press, Inc.
   10 Alice Street
   Binghamton, NY 13904-1580

Pediatric Physical Therapy
   Williams & Wilkins
   351 West Camden Street
   Baltimore, MD 21201-2436
   (quarterly)

Physical and Occupational Therapy in Geriatrics
  The Haworth Press, Inc.
  10 Alice Street
  Binghamton, NY 13904-1580
  (quarterly)

Physical and Occupational Therapy in Pediatrics
  The Haworth Press, Inc.
  10 Alice Street
  Binghamton, NY 13904-1580
  (quarterly)

Physical Therapy Forum
  Forum Publishing Co.
  251 West Dekalb Pike, Suite D-100
  King of Prussia, PA 19406
  (semimonthly)

Physical Therapy Today
  Williams & Wilkins
  351 West Camden Street
  Baltimore, MD 21201-2436
  (quarterly)

BOOKS

As with journals, there are many fine books from which to choose. The following list is only a small sampling of what's out there for the health fitness student and professional.

Arnheim, Daniel D. *Modern Principles of Athletic Training.* St. Louis: Times Mirror, 1989.

Bouchard, Claude. *Physical Activity, Fitness, and Health Consensus Statement.* Champaign, IL: Human Kinetics Publishers, 1993.

Cooper, Kenneth H. *The Aerobics Program for Total Well-Being.* New York: Bantam, 1982.

———. *Controlling Cholesterol* (1988).

———. *Dr. Kenneth Cooper's Antioxident Revolution* (1994).

———. *It's Better to Believe* (1995).

———. *Kid Fitness* (1991).

———. *New Aerobics for Women* (1988).

———. *Overcoming Hypertension* (1990).

———. *Preventing Osteoporosis* (1989).

———. *Running Without Fear* (1985).

Novich, Max M. *Training and Condition of Athletes.* Philadelphia: Lea & Febiger, 1970.

Shephard, Roy J. *Economic Benefits of Enhanced Fitness.* Champaign, IL: Human Kinetics Publishers, 1986.

———. *Fitness in Special Populations.* Champaign, IL: Human Kinetics Publishers, 1990.

Sorensen, Jacki. *Aerobic Lifestyle Book.* New York: Poseidon Press, 1983.

Valentine, Tom and Carol. *Applied Kinesiology: Muscle Response in Diagnosis, Therapy, and Preventive Medicine.* New York: Thorsons Publishing Group, 1985.